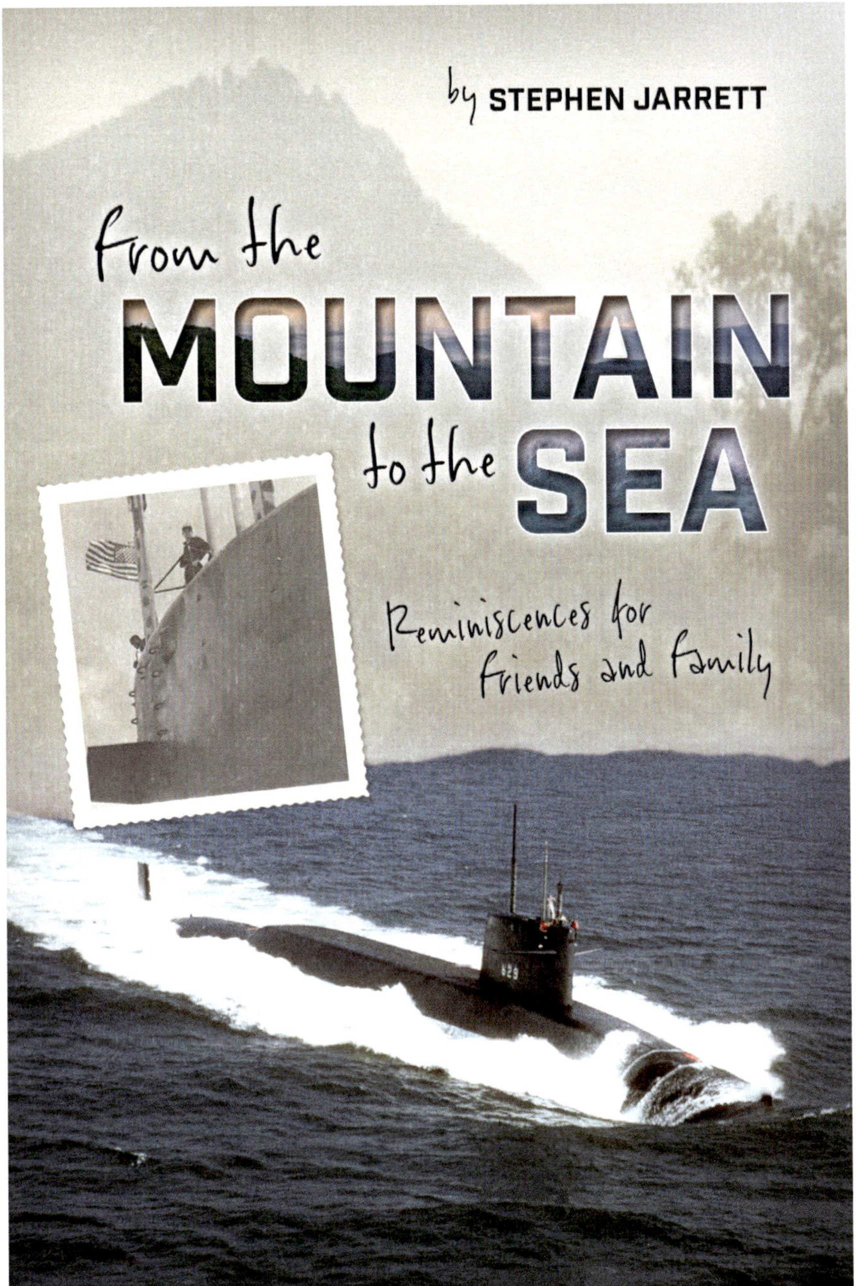

STONE TOWER PRESS

I0809502

From the Mountain to the Sea:
Reminiscences for Friends and Family

Stone Tower Press
7 Ellen Rd.
Middletown, RI 02842
stonetowerpress.com

Paperback ISBN: 979-8-9919831-5-0

Cover and text design by Amy Cole and Amy Landheer, JPL Design Solutions

Printed in the United States of America

This is a country boy's journey from a small Georgia town to command of a nuclear submarine with ten times the firepower of all bombs dropped during World War II. When you're at the foot of the mountain, it always looks insurmountable. However, as we journey along through life, if we are receptive and reflective we find out who we truly are inside and who God intended us to be. We also find out that we can climb the mountain and reach the top.

Currahee Mountain,
Stephens County, Georgia

CONTENTS

Aboard *USS Daniel Boone* (SSBN–629)

INTRODUCTION

The question seemed to always arise in my mind "Why are you taking time to write this?" There are a lot of other things that I might be spending my time doing. I've found that the more people I talk to about my life and experiences as well as their lives and experiences, the more important the stories of our past histories become. You'll find me talking a lot about my relatives, most of whom have already gone to be with the Lord. Some were great men and women, but they are easily now forgotten. Uncle Rudy was my favorite fishing buddy when I was 10 or 11. I never knew until much later that he was shot down over Germany in World War II and was a German POW for three years. In the following pages you will find a number of stories about my uncles in this memoir because, honestly, I had a lot of uncles! My mom had eight brothers and sisters. You have probably heard of the "Band of Brothers," a U.S. Army paratrooper group in World War II ("Easy" Company, 2nd Battalion, 506th Parachute Infantry Regiment of the 101st Airborne Division). Uncle Del Crowder was an instructor for them at Camp Toccoa in my hometown in Georgia. Their training facility was on Currahee Mountain. The name *Currahee* is Cherokee for "I stand alone." It is the last mountain in the chain of the Blue Ridge Mountains. He never mentioned it. Such was the nature of so many of his generation.

Once, I spoke to about 120 veterans in Toccoa, Georgia. They invited me to speak because I left our little town and eventually became a a nuclear submarine captain. With the many challenges in our world today, we need many more success stories of bravery, courage, and perseverance to teach our youth that it's not hopeless unless you give up. Many in the media today would say you have to be a particular race or ethnic group to succeed. But that is incorrect. When I was in grammar school, we didn't have indoor plumbing. I grew up with a loaded shotgun next to the front door and yet, we never saw any mass shootings in my high school. We have forgotten the words and deeds of great Americans of the past. You may think that you're nothing special and don't have anything to add—but you are wrong. You are unique. You need to tell your stories of success and failure. Tell your stories of faith. Tell your stories of life and death and the significance of the little things that kept you going when the times were tough—and still keep you going. If you do so, you will be surprised how valuable your stories and wisdom are to others

High School Graduation

Traveler's Rest

Traveler's Rest is located in the Tugaloo Valley which was formerly inhabited by the Cherokee Indians. This site was included in land granted to Major Jesse Walton in 1785. Walton was a Revolutionary War veteran who had fought at King's Mountain and a frontiersman who came to the Tugaloo Valley from North Carolina where he had been a settlement leader and a member of the State's Executive Council.

Although the Cherokees had withdrawn from the valley before Walton arrived, the Creeks to the south tried to resist the spread of settlements in northeast Georgia. Year after year, marauding Creeks forced the pioneers to gather in small forts or blockhouses and to urgently and 'humbly' appeal to the governor of Georgia for a 'Relief of men and ammuniton'. But the governor could not provide them with these needs, and he recommended that they turn, not to the State for help but to the other frontiersmen such as Walton's friend, General Elijah Clark.

Despite continued Indian attacks, the Tugaloo settlers farmed and established homes. During this troubled period, the Creeks mortally wounded Walton in the vicinity of Traveler's Rest. Indian Agent Joseph Martin wrote to Virginia Governor Patrick Henry from 'Tugaloo in Georgia, July 2, 1789' that the Indians 'made an attack on this quarter, killed and wounded several, among which was Major Walton, who is at my elbow ... I expect will expire in a few moments from this time.'

After his death, Walton's property passed on to his wife and children, one of whom was probably the first to build a dwelling at the site of the present Traveler's Rest. Mary Walton, his widow, died in 1800, and within the next decade his children began to leave the valley in pursuit of cheaper lands in the west. In 1813, they relinquished their claims on the land to Joseph Martin, Walton's son-in-law and perhaps the nephew of the Indian agent. Martin began the structure which was expanded later and is known today as Traveler's Rest.

As stagecoach and riverboat traffic increased in the Tugaloo Valley, the site gained considerable financial status as a crossroads. In 1818, Martin sold the site for $2000 to James R. Wyly. As a builder of the Unicoi turnpike and a commissioner to improve navigation on the Tugaloo River, Wyly must have recognized the value of the land. He enlarged Martin's house and probably opened it as an inn to accommodate the growing number of travelers to northeast Georgia.

In 1833 for $6000, Wyly sold several pieces of land, including the crossroads inn, to his neighbor Devereaux Jarrett. The son of Revolutionary War veteran of the same name, Jarrett was raised in Oconee County, South Carolina, and moved to the Georgia side of the Tugaloo in the early 1800's. A man of great enterprise, he operated a country store, a tavern, a post office, a blacksmithy, a tanyard, a cotton gin, a sawmill, a grist mill and a toll bridge, as well as a large plantation.

Since that time, restoration work and research have progressed steadily. Today visitors can see Traveler's Rest as it was in the mid-nineteenth century - the stagecoach inn and plantation house of an enterprising northeast Georgia planter and businessman.

use to be Jarrett Manor for 100 yrs.

Newspaper article about Jarrett Manor

1

DOWN BY THE RIVER

It was way out in the country;
no neighbors and no plumbing.

To say our house was in the country was an understatement. We were about a mile and a half from the nearest neighbor. There was a country dirt road that ran along the Tugaloo River that ended at our house on the top of the hill in the bend of the river. Our home was across the river from the intersection of the Chauga Creek and the Tugaloo River. The small community of Old Madison, South Carolina was on the other side of the water and we could sometimes hear the church bells from a small white church over there. In the past, there was an Indian burial mound close to that intersection on the South Carolina side of the river.

Country Living

We farmed, but only part-time. Dad had another job as a machinist full-time. When I was growing up we lived in an old farmhouse that was only heated by a wood-burning stove that had a flue connected to the chimney. My brother, Jack, is 17 years older than me so I don't remember when he lived at home with us. Jean, my sister, is four and a half years older than me so when she graduated from high school I was just starting high school.

My family owned the farm for many years before I was born but we didn't move there permanently until I was in the third grade. Our farm was 255 acres with about 70 acres of river bottom land that we farmed. Our home was on the top of the hill at the very end of the road. When I was in elementary school if you heard a car, either someone was coming to visit us or they were lost. We had a number of animals including cows, hogs, chickens, and hunting dogs. I always wanted a horse but never could convince my dad that it would be worthwhile and worth the money it would take to feed one.

Life was much simpler when I was growing up on the farm. We cut firewood frequently on Saturdays, and every day we had to feed all the animals, collect the eggs, and milk the cows. We also had a number of gardens and raised most of our food. Mom didn't have a job outside the home while I was in school. She canned vegetables all summer and worked the gardens. Even though we didn't have a lot of money, we always had enough and we had plenty to eat. We primarily grew corn on the farm to feed to the animals.

Every year, Mom would can about a 100 quarts of green beans and 100 quarts of tomatoes or tomato juice. We also had a huge chest freezer and froze corn, squash, okra, peas and other vegetables. There are a lot of peach orchards in North Georgia and we used to pick about 6 bushels of peaches a year from one of the orchards. For that endeavor we usually went to Royston, Georgia, the home town of baseball legend Ty Cobb. Many times the sister aunts would get together and have a canning or freezing party. We would dip the peaches in boiling water and the skins would fall off. Then Mom or one of the ladies would slice them up and pour sugar syrup on them and we'd freeze them in plastic bags. Eating some of them was one of my favorite treats growing up.

We usually also slaughtered a steer every year and had the butcher cut the meat and wrap it in freezer paper. He'd write on the outside of the paper what the meat was inside. The hogs we butchered were either frozen or smoked in our 100 year-old smoke house as ham, sausage, and bacon.

My dad, uncles, and grandfather would get together when it was getting cold outside in the fall and put a 55-gallon drum under where my swing hung on the sycamore tree in the front yard. They'd fill the drum with water and build a fire around it to heat it up. Our hog pen was up the drive way toward the log barn next to a huge oak tree about 5–6 feet in diameter. They would kill the hog and bring him down to the yard. They then tied his hind legs together and hoisted him on my swing limb above the boiling water in the drum. They'd dip him in the water to loosen up his bristles, lift him up and scrape off the hair. I guess some people today might call us "survivalists." We just called ourselves "country folks."

As I noted above, our smokehouse was probably a hundred years old. The timbers in the roof were hand-hewn. There were also gaps in the upper structure between the vertical siding boards. There was a dirt floor in the building and we had a metal grate on the dirt. We'd cut a hickory tree and build a fire in the grate. Dad would then throw some dirt on the coals and get them smoking. The hams and bacon and other meat was hung from wires from the cross beams above. We also had a huge box in the corner and some of the smoked meat was salted and stored there to cure.

In the yard we had fig trees, bunch grapes, plums, and a scuppernong vine that you walked under. We canned grape juice and Dad made scuppernong wine that tasted like nectar. The recipe was passed down from my grandfather, Mac Jarrett. Taking care of the animals took a lot of time and I helped Dad with the chores. We raised all of the corn that we fed the hogs and cows. Because we didn't have an operational corn picker, we had to pick it by hand. At age ten, I began to drive the tractor with the trailer on the back and help Dad pick up the corn from piles in the field. Dad picked it by hand and piled it up. When we had a trailer load, I'd sometimes get to drive it back from the field to the log corn crib. The crib was lined with hardware cloth so the varmint animals couldn't get the corn but that didn't stop them from trying. Sometimes Dad would catch a king snake and put him in the crib to keep the rodents down. It was also really effective in keeping us kids out of the crib!

As a result of driving the tractor and our 1951 Studebaker pickup, I learned to drive a stick shift transmission at age 10 or 11. I was driving the tractor when I was so small that I had to stand up to reach the clutch. We didn't have running water or indoor plumbing so we had a privy down the hill from the house. Our house sat on the top of a hill, and on one occasion I was driving the tractor with the trailer attached around the house to get down to where Dad was cutting firewood. The tractor started down the hill and I couldn't turn it back around toward where I wanted to go. Thank the Lord for the tree stump that stopped the tractor. I was on a direct path to hit the privy. The bad thing was that my sister and mom were both in it at the time!

I had another incident with firewood when I was in the third grade. It was a cold morning and my brother, Jack, was pitching firewood from the pile behind the house to the concrete steps in the breezeway. For some reason, I decided to go up the steps and into the house. With my hand on the top step Jack threw the stick of firewood and crushed the index finger on my left hand. He put me in the car and drove me to the emergency room in town about ten miles away. It was the fastest trip that I ever made on a dirt road. The last joint on that finger is still about half the length of the last digit on my right hand, but other than that I don't have any other issues with it.

Being out in the country, I was also very familiar with firearms. We hunted and fished all the time. I got my first shotgun when I was 10 and used to hunt frequently with my cousins, uncles, and by myself. We had one rule that remained in effect for many years. That rule was, "you kill it or catch it; you clean it." So I dressed all the rabbits and squirrels that I shot and we ate them. We had fried rabbit or squirrel and dumplings. I also had a rabbit box trap most of the time. I'd set them at night and in the morning frequently we'd have rabbit for supper the next day.

Living in the country may have been a hardship for some people but it never was for me. However, my dating life suffered because we didn't get a telephone until I was in the eleventh grade, but I still loved country life anyway. Many days and weekends were spent hunting squirrels and rabbits in the fall and winter. I spent many hours in the woods and on the river bank fishing with my uncles.

When we moved to the country in the late 1950s, it was still pretty primitive. We had a hand-dug well in the front yard with a bucket and windlass. It was about 70 feet deep. Remember, we didn't have running water; we had a privy down the hill for a bathroom. That wasn't too bad except at night or when the wasps decided to build a nest in it. I guess we were poor but just didn't know it. We certainly didn't feel that way.

The Sitting Room

Because we were in the bend of the Tugaloo River, we had two river access areas. On the front of the bend closest to the house, we were on the top of a hill. In the back bottoms we had another section of the river. The Russell's owned the property adjacent to us. In the back bottoms the river over many years had washed out a room-sized hole that we used to fish from. We even took some old rocking chairs down there and would sit in them when we fished. We called it the "sitting room." On one of our fishing trips with my Uncle Glenn, we were fishing there and a water snake swam up right at my feet and stuck his head up out of the water. Uncle Glenn grabbed a tree limb and quickly dispatched the snake with a swift swat.

We "borrowed" a short-horned bull from one of Dad's friends to get our cows in a family way. The bull was white and maroon. He was all spotted. He was also pretty feisty. He escaped from the barn and decided he liked freedom in the back bottoms. We couldn't catch him. However, Uncle Del Crowder was from Oklahoma and was a pretty good cowboy. He was also a paratrooper from the "Band of Brothers" of Toccoa. He brought his lasso rope over to the farm and was able to coach the bull to get within range and he lassoed him just like in the rodeo. I watched in amazement. My uncles were many-talented people. The bull did do his job and we returned him to his owner. So much for sex education on a farm.

Throughout my youth Traveler's Rest was called "Jarrett Manor." Several things that are not mentioned in this article. There was a huge wooden sign on Highway 123 giving directions to "Jarrett Manor" that was later replaced by the state with a "Traveler's Rest" sign. My Jarrett family held family reunions at Jarrett Manor outside on the grounds for many years. Later we also combined those with the Ramsey family in Jarrett/Ramsey reunions. There would be 50 or more people at these events. In the peak of the roof of the manor there were two lookout holes cut in the siding so that those inside would to be able to see attacking Indians or to be able to shoot from it if necessary.

A Snake in the Kitchen—and Others

When we first moved down to the country and area of north Georgia, we were much more in the woods than I had ever been before in my life. The house was an old home that was originally built with two separate sides having a road through the middle that a wagon was driven through like a garage. When we moved into the house it was about a 100 years old with hand hewn timbers in the roof. The doors weren't really tight since the previous renters had cats and had carved out holes in the doors for them to get in and out. We later plugged them up.

One morning, Mom got up to fix us breakfast and found a chicken snake in the kitchen. Dad took care of the snake with a .22 rifle and then we had breakfast. Not many people can say their dad shot a chicken snake in the kitchen.

My folks used to tell a story about me when I was very young. Back then I wore cowboy boots all the time. I also used to ride on the 1950 Ford tractor when Dad plowed and worked the bottom land around the river. Dad occasionally would find a snake in the field and if it ran into a hole, he would step on its tail and cut it in half with his pocket knife. I honestly can't remember when I didn't carry a pocket knife. I routinely did at 5 years old and still do at 74. I saw a little snake in the field and stepped on his head and promptly dispatched him with my pocket knife. Mom wanted the rules changed after that, but I don't remember her convincing dad to do so.

When I was a little guy, I slept on the roll-away folding bed in my parent's bedroom. We only had one other bedroom before we remodeled the home and that was my sister's. We had two big rock chimneys, one on each end of the house. During the summertime we put a metal cover over the fireplace in the bedroom because we didn't have any covers on the top. The chimney swifts used to nest in the top of the chimney. They'd fly over the house like fighter planes and dive down the chimney. They built small mud and leaf nests on the side of the chimney wall. One night we heard something drop down the chimney. Dad slowly pulled back the cover and there was a black snake laying on the fireplace floor. He had a chimney swift in his mouth and two more wrapped up in his tail. Dad was good at protecting us from the snakes.

Later, I walked around the house on the way to go fishing down at the bottom of the hill. There was a snake laying on a limb about 8 feet off the ground in one of our crape myrtles. Mom said, "Steve go get the rifle." So I brought the pump .22 out of the house and gave it to her. She took aim and fired three shots. All hitting the snake in rapid succession. You didn't want to mess with Mom.

Christmas in the Country

I know that we now think that Christmas is around the corner when we see Christmas trees being sold on vacant lots and at Lowes and other stores. However, when I was a teenager, it was different. We never bought a tree that I remember. When I was squirrel hunting or out in the woods, I'd look for one that was about the right size and height. Sometimes they weren't perfect, but that was what the long silver foil icicles were for, to fill in the blank spots. We had decorations that were decades old and we rarely bought any new ones. I'd take a hatchet and cut the tree down and lug it back home.

Summer Jobs

During my high school years I worked every summer for three years for Bowen and Watson Construction Company. I was the lowest of the low and I was paid minimum wage. It was good for me that almost every year they seemed to raise the minimum wage! However, it was good work and good experience. I did a number of jobs, mostly with a shovel. They needed someone to dig a huge hole with straight up sides for an installation at the telephone company. I was selected and went to work. The only issue was that at the end of the day the hole was so deep and the sides straight up that I couldn't get out of the hole. They had to bring me a ladder to get out!

We also built a new wing on the Lake Louise Baptist Conference Center on the second story of the facility. We had to pour a concrete beam over 100 feet long measuring 3 feet by about 2 feet. They didn't use the pumper trucks back then. When we started pouring the beam on the second floor roof, we had to complete it without stopping so there wouldn't be a weak place in the concrete. There were several of us working and we wheelbarrowed the concrete across the roof on a makeshift track of boards. The issue was that it was a hot summer day in Georgia and the roof was painted black. It must have been 110° on the roof. We poured all day until we got it finished.

I also was a brick mason's helper for one summer. We mixed the mortar and carried it up two stories to the mortar boards for the masons. I still remember it was 17 shovels of sand to 1 bag of mortar mix. One mason was too lazy to mix a little water with the mortar and stir it up if it got a little dry and stiff. He'd just scrape it off two stories high and loudly order some more. We also didn't have lifts to get the bricks up to the second story scaffolding. So we teamed up with a "pitcher" and "catcher" to toss the bricks up to the second floor. That was hard work! I went through a pair of leather gloves a week doing that work. The concrete blocks were even tougher. The bottom guy would grab them with two hands and raise them over his head as high as possible and the top guy would reach down and grab them. We certainly didn't need weight training for football practice! I learned a lot and later even built a brick wall for one of my friends at his house on Smith Street in downtown Charleston.

Southern Ingenuity and Fishing

After the Lake Hartwell reservoir was built and filled, we decided to put a floating dock in the water from which to fish. Dad and I built it up at the house and put four big blocks of Styrofoam under it. Then came the kicker, "how do we get it in the water?" We managed to get it on the trailer for the tractor and then got it down the old dirt road to the water's edge and actually got it floating. Dad went back to the house to launch Uncle Harold's small wooden fishing boat. I held the dock in place to keep it from floating away. I got an idea and since I had my bathing suit on anyway, I grabbed the rope to the dock and swam it around the point to where we were going to anchor it. When Dad got back with the boat, I already had it on the point. Then we built a ramp out to it and anchored it in the water with an old car engine block and two chains. It stayed there many years.

As a teenager, Uncle Rudy and I were fishing on the dock one afternoon. I was casting a MirrOlure minnow. I caught two walleyed pikes from the dock. One was about 4 pounds and the other was 6 pounds and 3 ounces. Because they had been stocked and were not native to the area, I took the bigger one and had it weighed. I found out later that if I had entered it on the other side of the lake, the South Carolina side, it would have been a state record for 3 years. My cousins, the Crowders, were running Portman Shoals Marina near Anderson, South Carolina. Uncle Del knew a good taxidermist and he had it mounted for me. It still hangs in my office after almost 60 years.

On another fishing trip, Uncle Rudy was fishing with me off the dock with a cane pole and a live minnow with a float. A white bass hit the minnow and the cane was long gone. We watched it from the dock and it made a huge loop out into the lake, but then started to come back around toward the dock. When it got close enough, Uncle Rudy cast a lure across the pole and hooked it. He was able to reel it in and land the two-pound white bass on the hook. It's the longest fish story in history!

Squirrel and Rabbit Fest

We had five huge pecan trees in our yard in Georgia. However, we never got any pecans. We were surrounded by forests on every side and the squirrels knew where we lived. One year my dad decided he was going to lower the squirrel population and get some pecans. He bought himself a small .22 caliber rifle with a scope and being a Marine, he was a good shot. He would take out a squirrel and feed him to his cats who lived close to the barn and crib. The cats also kept down the rodents in that area. At last count he'd harvested 83 squirrels. He still didn't get any pecans. I guess they multiplied faster than he subtracted.

We also had a lot of rabbits around the house. Dad bought 50 cabbage plants to put in one of our several gardens. The rabbits thought it was a smorgasbord and moved in for dinner. They ate all 50 plants down into the ground. Dad was working at Sangamo Electric that manufactured the electric meters for the side of houses. He invited some of his buddies to come over one weekend for a rabbit hunt and they brought their dogs. They took 10 rabbits right around the house. I don't remember if we tried to grow cabbage again. Dad's friends invited us to a "rabbit mull." I guess that is Southern slang for a big pot of Brunswick stew that included rabbit. They had a huge cast iron pot and a wood fire around it. The stew had corn, tomatoes, and some other "secret" ingredients and tasted very good. I've eaten Brunswick stew in a number of places and restaurants. None of them tasted the same. The recipe must be passed down with the other family treasures. The best I've had is at a small BBQ restaurant called the BBQ Shack in Toccoa, Georgia.

We attended the First Methodist Church in Toccoa, Georgia while I was growing up. I also sang in the "Wesley Singers," a youth choir while I was in high school. Our youth group at church was very active as well. In the Methodist Youth Fellowship (MYF), I had a number of friends. We lived way out in the country but most of my MYF friends lived in town. So they attended Toccoa High School but I attended Stephens County High School. My first encounter with salvation came when a Lay Witness Mission group came to our church.

I was also in the 4-H Club while I was a teenager. Because I raised chickens and sold eggs, it was easy for me to participate in the poultry part of the 4-H Club. I also went to the summer camp at Camp Rock Eagle in Eatonton, Georgia and at one point, I won the District Poultry Award. I had a number of regular customers for my eggs and sold about 9 dozen a week. That was quite entrepreneurial for a young fellow. I bought my own chicken feed and got the young chicks from the county agent, Mr. Newman. I also raised a Herford steer, named Curley. We had other cows and hogs too so it wasn't really a stretch. I showed Curley at the county fair and I remember one of the negative things was giving him a bath and brushing him to get him ready for the fair. He weighed in at about a thousand pounds (1000) when he was mature. We were a farm so we didn't raise chickens and steers for just showing. After about a year of egg laying the chickens' egg production started to taper off, so we would harvest all 25 and put them in the freezer and I'd start over with 25 new chicks.

Midshipman,
U.S. Naval Academy

Midshipman Third Classman (Sophomore)

2

U.S. NAVAL ACADEMY

It's a big jump from "big man on campus" in High School to being the lowest of the low.

Annapolis, Maryland, the home of the United States Naval Academy, was on a chart that I made in grammar school. I guess my Dad planted that seed early. I actually got the congressional nomination to attend the school in the eleventh grade and had to tell them that I hadn't graduated yet from high school. I did get it again the next year from Representative Phil Landrum. It probably didn't hurt that I took every math, physics, and chemistry course that my school offered and was the Valedictorian and Star Student. I also played football for four years and wrestled on our school team for four years. When my appointment letter came in the mail, I was in town and my Dad brought the letter to me.

Military Family and Plebe Summer

When it came time for me to report for Plebe Summer detail in Annapolis, I caught a train from Toccoa to Washington, DC. From there I rode a bus to Annapolis, Maryland. I had a lot of friends in Toccoa from my church group, my sports teams, and from school. There were over 100 people at the train station to see me leave. I didn't make it home for over six months. At 18, it was quite a change. I'd only seen the ocean twice as a youngster when our family took a short infrequent vacation and had gone to South Georgia for several days. My brother Jack also took me on a fishing trip out of Panacea, Florida. We caught over 100 pounds of fish and brought them back in several coolers.

With the Vietnam War in full swing, my draft lottery number came up at 34 out of 365. That's the only lottery that I ever won. We also took a battery of tests in high school for the U.S. Air Force and they rigorously tried to recruit me to enlist. I was the first Navy person in my family. All my uncles were Army Air Corps or Army infantry and Dad was a Marine from 1928–1934. Two of my uncles were shot down on bombing runs in Europe. Uncle Rudolph Purcell was a POW for three years and only weighed 90 pounds when he returned home after being liberated. Uncle Kyle Purcell was able to escape to Sweden after being shot down and avoided capture. He was smuggled back to England in a black boat at night. He was on the first bombing run of Peenemünde (the German Army Research Center, or *Heeresversuchsanstalt Peenemünde*, where German rockets and other weapons were developed) and the first bombing raid on Berlin. Uncle Kyle was a belly gunner on a B-17, that's the guy who rarely got out alive if the plane crash landed. He received a Bronze Star. Uncle Glenn was in the infantry in North Africa with General Patton and was a part of the Sicily invasion and Uncle Harold was not successful in flight training and worked in hospitals until the end of the war.

Mom also had four sisters. Aunt Loyce married Uncle Guy Seymour. He was on the Normandy Invasion and won a Bronze Star for the Sicily Invasion. Aunt Louella married a paratrooper from Camp Toccoa, Del Crowder. As noted in the last chapter, Uncle Del was an instructor for the "Band of Brothers" from Currahee Mountain. Aunt Dot married Uncle Dewey Camp, who served in Panama and was a U.S. Army Air Corps veteran of World War II. Aunt Robbie married Uncle Harrison, who wasn't in uniform due to medical issues.

As noted above, my dad, Max Jarrett, was a Marine 1928–1934. During this time he went to Haiti on one of our other excursions. The Marines were in Haiti from 1915–1934. My Brother, Jack Jarrett, was in the Air Force and was a radar operator in Turkey on the Soviet border for two years.

When I married Carolyn Elaine Crouse in 1981, I didn't know the extent of military service in her family. Her father, Dr. Vance Crouse, was a Burma, India and China vet from World War II and a Korean War vet. In Korea he was the doctor, dentist and veterinarian in his Army company all at the same time. He retired as a full colonel in the U.S. Air Force. Elaine's Uncle Ray Kaltreider, was on the battleship *Oklahoma* (BB-37) when it was capsized after being attacked by the Japanese at Pearl Harbor on December 7, 1941. Fortunately, he was a good swimmer. He survived and rescued a number of other sailors but this resulted in burns and scars on his back from the burning oil on the water. Ray lied about his age and actually enlisted in the Navy at the age of 14. He was an orphan. Ray stayed in the Navy and actually went from being a seaman to being a commander and got command of a ship. Ray's son, Dan, was a Marine officer in Vietnam and passed away from prostate cancer from exposure to Agent Orange in Vietnam.

Hazing—is it teaching leadership or just being mean to junior people?

As plebe midshipmen we were required to report early for Plebe Summer before classes started for the academic year. It was like some other schools call "hell week," but it lasted more than a month. We were brought down to ground zero, by being required to run everywhere we went, bracing up in the halls and never looking around but always straight ahead. I was in the hardest major at the academy—-electrical engineering. That would have been difficult at any university but there, it was excruciating. We had numerous things that we had to memorize on a daily basis and be ready to repeat them to any upper classmen. If we were asked what's for the evening meal, we were required to repeat verbatim the menu that was posted. We did what was known as "chow call" on a rotating basis.

Whoever had the "duty" on the watch bill, had to stand at the end of the hall and loudly shout out the menu and the time to the formation for each meal.

There is a lot written today about hazing incidents in colleges. Not so much when I was at the Naval Academy. It was accepted to some level. My first class squad leader told his buddies that he was going to kick me out of the Navy. He evidently didn't know my family. He was also from New York. It was standard procedure that when you were given demerits, you were placed on "Plebe Morning Workouts" to work off the demerits. When you got on those workouts you had to muster at 0530 (5:30 AM) and run with a group of other plebes led by one of the upper classmen. We'd run 4–5 miles and do exercises. Usually, most of the plebes were off these workouts by the half-year point. I was on them until June Week at graduation.

My company had a number of varsity sports freshmen and jocks who were in great shape. We'd start off the run and begin to push the upper classmen to a faster and faster pace. There were a number of times that they didn't finish first at the end of the run.

My first class squad leader at one point told me to go out and "run 8 miles." So I did—in 71 minutes. I reported back to his stateroom and said "I'm done. Anything else you want me to do?" I admit that is a bit of a sassy answer. He drew a circle with chalk on the blackboard in the hall and made me stand with my nose in that circle until evening meal formation. The academy also has a tradition that on one night before graduation, the plebes become first class and the first class become plebes. You get to pick your first class person. It usually involves some innovative way to ask your choice to "come around." My first classman's nickname was "Mover." So at the evening meal I grabbed a pitcher of milk and hit him square in the face with a deluge while yelling, "Come around Mover!" Needless to say, I paid for that action. When I got back to my room, he piled all of my uniforms in the shower and made me stand on them and turn on the water. On "half-way night" when he was supposed to be my plebe for the night, he refused to do most of what I told him to do. He was evidently all bluff and no do.

Overall, my plebe year was a real wake-up call to a small town boy from north Georgia. Academically, I knew I could make it, but the hazing and the nastiness from the upper classmen was a real surprise. However, one thing that I did helped some. I joined the Antiphonal Choir at the chapel. I sang tenor and through being a member of that choir, I got to go on several trips with the choir. We went to Scarsdale, New York and sang in a church there. In the chapel at the Naval Academy we sang from the balcony in the back of the chapel. The Glee Club processed into the chapel during services but we just assembled in the balcony and sang from there. It also gave me a chance to get out of Bancroft Hall for choir practice once a week. We also made a trip to Washington, DC and I can now say I've sung tenor in the National Cathedral!

Whenever we were in the Bancroft Hall we were required to "chop," jog with our chins in, and look straight ahead. We were not allowed to speak unless spoken to and we had to address every upperclassman as "Sir." During all meals we had to sit erect and "brace up." That meant that we had to push our chins in as far as possible and eat "Square meals." That meant that you didn't use your fork to bring food directly to your mouth. It went up in front of you to the level of your mouth and then straight in. It's a learned procedure. The other issue was that we had a number of things that we had to memorize every day. They were such things as the menu for the next meal (verbatim), the officer of the day, the football schedule, and many other unrelated things. We had a small blue book, called *Reef Points*, with quotations in it about all the things in the "yard" around the campus. We also had a number of quotations and even one about the milk at the dinner table. That one was called "How's the cow?" When asked that you grabbed the milk carton to see how much was left. If it was 50% you would say, "She walks, she talks, she's full of chalk. The cow is prolific to the 50th degree." I don't know who came up with that.

There was another issue when you met an upperclassman. They could "drop" you to do pushups for almost any reason whatsoever for 72 pushups, because I was in the Class of '72. It didn't mean that only one could do it. If there were three there, each could drop you for 72 pushups. Also, it didn't mean that they could only do it inside the Bancroft Hall quarters. They could also do it outside. I did get pretty good at doing pushups.

"Summer Cruise

At the Naval Academy, midshipmen took a "summer cruise" aboard a Navy ship every summer or went to some other type of military training. After plebe year, my first summer cruise was on an amphibious surface ship out of Norfolk going to Europe. We docked in Hamburg, Germany and it was quite a bit for a country boy from Toccoa to get a handle on. I had taken a year of German, so at least I could order some food at the restaurants. I do remember several of us getting together to go out to eat and ordering a Coke. They took it off the shelf warm and popped the cap and set it down in front of me.

The amphibious ship was designed with a huge space in the center, the well deck, that was flooded when they ballasted the ship down and opened the back to launch the landing craft out for a troop landing. They performed that operation for us to watch. It was interesting, but I preferred a ship designed to sink more than once so I looked at submarines the next year.

I also made it to Copenhagen, Denmark on that summer cruise. Some things really impress an 18 year old teenager from north Georgia who, basically, had never been anywhere.. As I was walking down the street in Copenhagen there was a full-sized picture in one of the store windows. It was of a fully nude good looking woman. I never did buy anything but was impressed with the advertisement. I don't remember what they were advertising.

"Youngster Year"

After plebe year when you became a third classmen, you didn't have any of the same requirements as a plebe. We also didn't participate in any of the hazing of the new plebes. It was refreshing to be out from under the gun. We started with 1400 plebes; only 981 graduated. Most of the attrition was during plebe year. Obviously, the academics also took out a considerable number of midshipmen.

Flight Training

After my sophomore year everyone went to flight training in Pensacola, Florida. We actually got to go up in the planes and fly them with an instructor. In the T-34, I did well and had a good time. When they shifted to the T-28 which was much more powerful and faster, my instructor wanted to do acrobatics and pretend to dogfight another plane. I got so sick that I threw up all over the cockpit. I guess my flight training was beneficial in at least teaching me what my capabilities were—and were not. We also did a helicopter assault on one occasion and I kept thinking that helos don't really fly—they beat the air into submission!

As a "First Class Mid," I chose to go on a submarine patrol on the USS *Thomas Jefferson* (SSBN–618). We met the submarine in Rota, Spain and that was also an interesting part of the journey. Some of my buddies and I planned to go by train to a beach on the Spanish Riviera, but we never made it there. We did go to a bull fight in Seville, Spain. It was a bloody affair. I didn't know that they killed the bulls with swords. You kind of wanted to pull for the bulls after a while.

On patrol aboard the submarine, we were ordered to execute a test missile launch and I was allowed to be in the missile control center for the shot. It was very interesting and probably a factor in me going into the submarine force after graduation.

Designated Academic Majors

I was in the first class at the Naval Academy to get "designated majors." Up until that time everyone had basically the same curriculum and ended up with a Bachelor of Science in Military Science. They offered 24 different majors and I chose Electrical Engineering. In high school I'd been offered a full scholarship to Georgia Tech to study chemistry. I had already pre-enrolled and paid my first housing fee when I received the appointment to the Naval Academy. I didn't think chemistry would be nearly as applicable to a Navy career as electrical engineering. That is why I decided to switch to "EE" as a major.

Second Class Year

As a member of the first class of the Naval Academy to have designated majors, I was in the first group of electrical engineers to graduate. Of the 80 midshipmen who had picked "EE" as their major, only 28 graduated in that field. It was brutal, to say the least. My junior year as a "Second Class" was especially hard for me. One semester I had 21 credit hours and a boatload of physics courses. I actually pulled an "all-nighter" once a week for the entire first semester trying to get the homework done and learn the material for my courses. I do especially remember one "Electricity and Magnetism" course. For my final exam I had to memorize 600 formulas. So I memorized the list and made a "B" on the exam. Of course, I can't remember any of them now. The midshipmen called the "Electricity and Magnetism" courses "Black Magic I and Black Magic II".

Having done really well in high school, I was not accustomed to grades as low as they were when they were passed out in the Semiconductor Physics course. We'd take an exam and the "average" grade would be 25, not 85. At the end of the semester, the professor added the grades together for one's grade. He didn't average them out, he just added them together. I made a "B" in that course. Also we had to do a project. That was in 1971, so computers were much more basic than they are now. I actually built a desktop computer from scratch and made it work. Admittedly, it wasn't a very good one but it worked. After my first year in Electrical Engineering they actually made that same professor the head of the department.

Nuclear Power Interview

In my senior year at the Naval Academy, I was toying with the idea of being a Marine Corps officer. The Vietnam War was still going, but it was winding down. There were a number of displays in the Rotunda at Bancroft Hall with the pictures of the fallen alumni. My dad said that he would prefer that I choose another path. As an electrical engineer, I was asked to go for an interview in Washington, DC with Vice Admiral Rickover for the nuclear power program. His reputation greatly preceded him and we heard stories about classic interviews he conducted and chairs with one leg shorter than the other for the applicants to sit in. Admiral Rickover personally interviewed every candidate.

My GPA as a junior with all of the physics courses for the Electrical Engineering major dropped me off the Dean's List (3.50), but I still graduated with a 3.01 overall GPA. As I entered Admiral Rickover's office on the day of the interview he began to scream and yell at me. I do remember the word "stupid" being used about my grade point average dropping. We'd been told by the aide that our primary goal was to get into the office as quickly as possible and to sit in the straight backed wooden chair in front of Admiral Rickover. I almost made it. I made it to the chair just as Admiral Rickover told me to get out of the room. So I walked around the chair and went back out. I was a little rattled because I'd never had a vice admiral scream at me. They put me in a small room with a desk and I sat there the rest of the day. I rode the bus back to Annapolis, but was told to come back the next day for another interview. I used the day to pick out which conventionally—powered surface ship that I wanted to be assigned to—a a DLG, a guided missile destroyer. I took the bus ride back to Annapolis and was much more resolved the next day. The turning point came when I saw Admiral Rickover leave his office in a wrinkled gray suit and go to the head after one of the other interviews. He was a short man with a head of white hair. At that point I said to myself, "either he picks me or not, but I'll not be intimidated by the interview." During my second interview he was quite civil and talked to me without screaming. I have to admit, I was surprised that I got selected after all.

Navy Sports (Making sure the most important things stay priorities.)

At the Naval Academy everybody had to play a sport, either intramural or varsity. I played battalion football and rugby and also field ball—it's a lot like lacrosse but slightly less violent. Our battalion football team did really well and became the Brigade champions two years in a row. That was quite a stretch from my high school football team that only won one game and lost nine in my senior year. One consolation was that we beat Commerce High School 7–6 and I tackled the runner on their extra point attempt. The only award for being brigade champions was that you got to wear some numbers on your Navy bathrobe. I liked rugby too. It was basically football without pads. Since I was a linebacker in high school I was very familiar with tackling. I remember one game that the other team broke free and I was the only defender standing between the man with the ball and the goal. I did a classic tackle putting my head in his stomach and lifting his feet off the ground.

One other event happened during my rugby career that greatly affected my future. During the last game of the season, I turned to walk off the field after the game and caught my cleats in the grass. I heard something pop and felt extreme pain in my left knee. Later that day my knee was swollen up bigger than my head. I found out that I had torn the medial meniscus. I was scheduled to have surgery during spring break. At Navy we also had physical fitness tests routinely. If you didn't pass their requirements, you were put on remedial workouts. I was scheduled for a fitness test before my surgery. They would not excuse me. So I taped my knee up tightly so that it wouldn't bend and ran the mile and a half stiff legged and passed anyway. I failed to tell my parents that I was having surgery and they were a bit surprised to get a call from the Navy hospital telling them that I was out of surgery and doing fine.

Having an injury like a knee surgery can be career destroying. One of my classmates and friends got his knee torn up badly during the Navy vs Texas football game. He was on both the varsity football team and the varsity baseball teams. After the injury the Navy medical review boards determined he was no longer physically qualified for unrestricted line duty. That meant that he could not have a normal career path and eventually command a ship or higher command. He was forced to go to supply officer school after Navy graduation and became a restricted line officer. One of my first roommates at the academy was on the varsity tennis team and also got injured and was also classified as restricted line.

After graduation, I drove my red MGB-GT back to Georgia with my friend Guy Brown from Texas. Sadly, he was killed in a helicopter crash in the Mediterranean a few years later. Guy had a different background than I did and he may have been a bit surprised when he got to our house in the country. I do remember breakfast the next day. Mom fixed homemade biscuits and gravy which was a staple at our house, along with eggs and ham, bacon or sausage most of the time. As the biscuits went around the table Guy took one and politely passed them to me. As normal I took two and split them and put gravy on them. He took a look and got another one and followed suit. I remember that one year before I left for Annapolis we killed and butchered seven hogs and smoked or cured them in our smoke house. Having enough to eat at our house was never an issue.

My dad got to drive my MG while I was home and I still remember his comment. "Your car sits really low to the ground, but it will run like a scalded dog." That's north Georgia slang for he really liked it.

Nuclear Power School—Electrical Engineer to Nuclear Engineer (You may never be finished learning new things.)

After graduation I was detailed (assigned) to temporary duty in Atlanta at the Navy recruiting station for three months while I waited for my class to start at the Navy Nuclear Power School at Mare Island, California. Uncle Harold Purcell lived in Atlanta and I was able to get a room from him during my time at the recruiting station. When it came time to leave for California, I packed everything I owned into a cruise box except my stereo speakers and amplifier and shipped the cruise box to California. I put my stereo and speakers in the back seat of my MG and drove across the country from Georgia to California. It was quite a trip for a young fellow just out of college. My mom had a map posted in the kitchen on the refrigerator and I would check in every evening and she would mark my location on the map. It took me about five days to drive from Georgia to California alone. I remember going past the meteor crater and detouring to see it and the Grand Canyon.

When I got to the Grand Canyon, I found out that I had a problem. I was almost out of gas and there were no gas stations open. I started back to the interstate about 25 miles away and put the car in neutral and let it coast. I'd slow down going up the hills and gain speed going down, but I coasted almost 25 miles to the first gas station!

When I arrived in Vallejo, California I rented a small apartment and found a Christian college group to get involved with pretty quickly. About two weeks after getting there, a man in a pickup truck with no insurance made an illegal left turn and hit me almost head-on in my MG totaling the car. He had a tire on top of the cab that wasn't tied down and it barely cleared the top of my car. I climbed out the window of my car and sat down on the pavement. The policeman drew a chalk circle around me on the road. I told him that I didn't get thrown from the car but climbed out. The impact on my left knee left me on crutches for two weeks.

Nuclear power school was more of the same type of education and training for me after graduating with a degree in Electrical Engineering—hard courses and lots of homework! However, I made it through and did ok. After six months of Nuclear Power School I was off to Idaho Falls, Idaho for nuclear prototype training for another six months. I was assigned to the A1W reactor plant. That was the aircraft carrier plant. There were actually five reactors at the site. It was a three-hour bus ride out to the prototype site each way and we were not allowed to drive. I asked one of the instructors what the parking meters were for at the site and was told that they were to plug your car into in the winter time to keep it from freezing. It gets really cold in Idaho in the winter! We worked on three-day shifts so I usually slept in the bunk room for three days at a time while working 60–70 hour weeks. It was a brutal time.

My buddies were assigned to the submarine nuclear prototypes, but for some reason I got sent to the aircraft carrier plant. Each of the prototypes had cooling towers where water was sprayed to remove the heat from the reactor plant since none of them had propulsion systems. There would be a slight mist over the submarine plants but not so over A1W, the aircraft carrier plant. There were two independent reactors at my facility. One was the older carrier, *Enterprise,* and the newer one was the *Nimitz.* My carrier plant was also probably ten times the power of the submarine plants. Because they were trying to deplete the *Nimitz*'s core to observe what the "end of life" criteria for the nuclear fuel was going to be like, we ran at 100% power all the time. Over our cooling tower there was a huge column of steam shooting five hundred feet into the air. We used to joke that we made it rain every Friday and it seemed to follow that pattern pretty closely.

One of my friends at the prototype was married . One day my roommate, Joe Brady and my friend and his wife and I went fishing in one of the canals out in the middle of a desolate field. They had a dog named Andy who was a white cocker spaniel with brown spots. Andy decided to roll in the cow paddies out in the field and came back a rather green mess. Obviously he was a city dog. They washed him off in the canal before we could come home. It was a very successful fishing trip for me but not so much for the other two guys. We were next to each other on the bank and were fishing with identical small spoon lures. I caught three steelhead trout and a 21-inch brown trout, but nobody else caught anything. They almost made me walk back with Andy. I told them my Uncle Rudy would say that they weren't holding their mouth right.

At the end of six months of prototype training we had to take a knowledge level written test and pass a panel of three instructors giving an interview to each of us. I did fine on the written test. When it came to my interview, one of the three panel members said I was deficient, so I failed. You were given two chances to pass or you were out of the program and sent out to the fleet. The executive officer sat as one of the members of my second board. The thing that I remember about that board is that he looked out the window in sheer boredom for the entire board. I don't think he looked at me once. He failed me on my second board. Because it was "two and you're out," I prepared to go home. I had another roommate in addition to Joe Brady. His name was Chuck Lusky. Chuck also was failed on his second board. The hardest part of the whole thing was I had to call my dad in Georgia and tell him that I'd failed out of prototype training.

The commanding officer of the prototype facility was a Naval Academy graduate named Captain Hughes. I was told to "come around" and talk to him. At the Academy, plebes are asked to "come around" and be quizzed by upper classman sometimes while you are hanging from the closet clothes bar because someone else was making you do that. He didn't make me do that, but he did have me come to his office and be quizzed personally by him for two weeks. Everybody else graduated and left for submarine school or the fleet. I was the senior class for two weeks. After that I had my unheard of third board. There was no way I was going to fail that after the Captain's intervention. After graduating, I drove from Idaho to New London, Connecticut for the Submarine Officer Basic Course. My friends were surprised to see me when I started the class two weeks late!

Submarine Officer Basic School ("Nuclear Submarining 101")

In New London Connecticut I found a top floor apartment for rent that was furnished for a reasonable amount. That was not a long course like Idaho so I had more time to get out and do some things in the local area. After the course I moved to Charleston, South Carolina and lived in the Bachelor Officer Quarters for a while. I had no furniture and not many other possessions at that time.

After a while Joe Brady and I got an apartment together. It worked out rather well because he was on a different schedule than I was and was on USS *Daniel Boone* (SSBN-629) while I was on USS *Von Steuben* (SSBN-632). So we both had the apartment to ourselves while the other guy was at sea and shared the expenses.

I once came home from patrol and there was a large number of silver platters and other silver stacked in the living room. It looked like someone was getting all the valuables together to rob the place. One thing that I haven't mentioned was that Joe's girlfriend was a semiprofessional golfer and she was really good. She was even better than Joe and he was a really good golfer too. Joe and Peggy had decided to get married and the silver was all of her awards from winning golf tournaments. So as she prepared to move in, I prepared to move out. I found a small house out in West Ashley that was brick and had a two-car garage separate from the house. I purchased my first house for about $21,000 and moved into it. The house was on Mulmar Street and had three bedrooms. It was fine for me and after a while I got a roommate to share the expenses. He was the navigator on the opposite crew from me on the same submarine. It worked out well because I had someone to watch over the house while I was gone and he had a house all to himself when he was in port and I was gone.

Because the house also had a detached two car garage I could store my car inside while I was at sea. I took advantage of the second stall to build a catamaran sailboat that I had fun with for many years. The two pontoons were made of block Styrofoam that I was able to carve into the right shape and cover with fiberglass cloth and epoxy paint. It was blue and had a deck constructed of plywood with center boards made from mahogany. I bought a 24-foot aluminum mast and after the boat's eventual demise, I've used the mast as a flagpole in my yard for a number of years.

Holy Loch, Scotland

Alisa Craig
Island, Scotland

Receiving Submarine Dolphins Pin

3

JUNIOR OFFICER TOURS

It's all about learning the ship systems, the operations, and your job.

Holy Loch, Scotland

My first submarine after graduation was out of the submarine base that the U.S. had in Holy Loch, Scotland. It was USS *Von Steuben* (SSBN–632 Gold). The SSBN rotation was three months in and three months out. The Blue crew would relieve us and we would fly back to the states. The submarine tender was docked in the Holy Loch and we would be tied up to it for about 30 days during turnover and refit. We would then go to sea through the Firth of Clyde into the North Sea. Dunoon at Holy Loch was a quaint little Scottish town with a number of bars for the sailors. The best part for me were the fish and chips vendors on the street corners. They sold fried fish and fries and wrapped them in a local newspaper. I got really scared a couple of times because we had to catch a cab to get to town. There is nothing more frightening than being in a cab on the wrong side of the road going really fast in the driving rain and seeing the headlights of an on-coming car coming over the hill in front of you. Thank goodness I didn't try to drive there!

In the picture, the submarine tender is anchored in the channel. The floating dry dock is anchored to the left. There is a walkway out to the ship in the middle of the loch from the tender on the right. I did six three-month patrols out of Holy Loch. One 30-day refit, I remember that it rained every day we were there. It never rained down in Scotland.

It only rained sideways! I had several pairs of wool pants that I only wore in Scotland after I once went topside in a pair of double-knit pants and had to look down to see if I had any pants on at all!

We were continuously training for upcoming operations and exams. Every man on board had a qualification card for his next qualification or position. The enlisted men were qualifying for their silver dolphins pin and the officers were working for their gold dolphins pin. Every enlisted man had to learn how to stop flooding in every compartment regardless of their work specialty. We'd see nuclear machinist mates in the torpedo room finding the valves for flooding down the torpedo tubes and torpedo men in the engine room finding the valves for the main sea water system. Everybody was assigned to damage control teams. This generated some interesting announcements over the 1MC (intercom system) during casualty drills or true casualties. One was "Away the CAT team to Machinery Two." The CAT stood for Casualty Assistance Team. Machinery Two was the compartment. The second in command, the executive officer, was in charge at the scene of the casualty such as fire, flooding or other emergencies. You got good at running breakneck speed from where ever you were to the scene to help with the casualty while you dodged the valve handles sticking out in the Missile Compartment.

The gold dolphin pin for the officers was an extremely difficult qualification to achieve. As a nuclear trained officer you had to first qualify to operate the reactor plant as Engineering Officer of the Watch (EOOW). This meant learning all the systems, procedures and casualty actions for operating the plant safely. Weapons officers had their own qualification for gold dolphins, but all officers except the supply officer had to qualify as Diving Officer, Officer of the Deck and Duty Officer in port. Both officers and enlisted crewmen were checked frequently for progress and tracked continuously on their qualification progress. Many casualty drills were required to give every person the opportunity to become proficient at all the different positions and responsibilities. We also held qualification boards for final certifications and made sure we had award ceremonies to congratulate the successful completion of the qualifications. My gold dolphins were presented to me by the Squadron Commander and I still have that picture in my office. As part of the "Zumwalt Navy" at that time (so-called after then-Chief of Naval Operations Admiral Elmo R. Zumwalt, known for his progressive "Z-gram" messages disseminated throughout the Navy to deal with personnel issues), I also have a mustache in that photo. The officer behind me is Mark Perreault, who was my running mate on my first ship.

The Firth of Clyde was really deep but the U.S. ships were not allowed to dive there. However, not so with the British subs. I remember going to sea and spotting a periscope in the channel ahead that didn't belong to us. The British submarine base was at Faslane, Scotland.

I qualified for and received my gold dolphins as a qualified submarine officer in 1975 on USS *Von Steuben* (SSBN–629 Gold). I served there for three years in positions as Electrical Officer, Reactor Controls Officer and as Damage Control Assistant and Auxiliary Division Officer. That was a pretty common rotation. Junior officers got to learn new jobs pretty frequently. About the time you became comfortable with the division job, you'd get rotated to a different position and learn a new part of the ship and new equipment.

As Electrical Officer you operated and maintained two 2000 KW turbine generators powered by steam, motor generators that converted DC to AC and AC to DC. We had a 126-cell battery and each cell weighed about 1000 pounds without the fluid. We also had all the switching systems to power everything on the ship. The Damage Control and Auxiliary Division officer operated all the hydraulics and atmosphere control systems. That included two huge electrolytic oxygen generators that converted distilled water to oxygen and hydrogen. If they didn't work, we could not stay submerged for very long. The two electrolytic oxygen generators charged the oxygen banks. We routinely bled oxygen into the ship with a front and back oxygen bleed station at about 120 standard cubic feet per hour rate. Mixing pure oxygen and hydrogen is always a dangerous operation and one of our oxygen generators had an explosive failure on one patrol. It was quickly contained and no one was injured.

While I was the Damage Control Assistant (DCA) and in charge of the Auxiliary Division, also called the "A gang," One of my sailors didn't like to wear socks. After about the third or fourth time of being chewed out by the XO for his appearance, I made a deal with the young man. He took a pair of socks and cut off the feet and stuffed the top part down into his boondocks. So he looked like he had socks on but you couldn't tell that the feet part was missing. It was a perfect solution and got both him and me off the hook with the XO.

I served as the Main Propulsion Assistant (MPA) and machinery division officer on USS *James Monroe* (SSBN–622) after my tour on USS *Von Steuben*. I picked up Monroe in the shipyard during a refueling overhaul. Sea time was strenuous, but overhaul was in shift work. At one point I worked 37 days in a row without a day off. I wasn't married back then and I picked the boat up in the shipyard in Kittery, Maine in Portsmouth Naval Shipyard. After we got the new reactor core installed and all of the shielding and other systems closed up, we did an initial startup. I was the initial criticality Engineering Officer of the Watch. The initial startup is an essential procedure because with a new core it's difficult to determine at which point the reactor will go critical. We approached it safely, pulling the control rods a small amount at a time and waiting for the nuclear reaction to occur. The reactor went critical and we got ready to go on sea trials. You don't get to install a new reactor core very often since they last for over 25 years of normal cruising.

At the beginning of a shipyard overhaul the two crew ballistic missile submarines combine crews to one crew for the shipyard period. At the end of the shipyard we split crews again into Blue and Gold, but there is a period where we have part of one crew and part of the other. As the Gold crew Main Propulsion Assistant and Machinery division officer, I was designated as the sea trials coordinator for the in water trials to test everything after the shipyard period. We were scheduled for a three day at sea period. I worked the schedule really hard and had to coordinate with a small surface chase ship. It was really important for the safety chase ship to be where we needed him to be when we got there. I provided a detailed schedule for them with locations and times. However, one final item probably sealed the deal. After getting to know the captain of the chase ship from a number of meetings, I went out and purchased a fifth of his favorite Scotch. He was Johnny on the Spot for the entire sea trials. We were the first submarine to finish all the three-day sea trial requirements in just two days. Sometimes it takes a little out of the box thinking to get to where you want to go. There are many instances of that in my career. The first step is usually to enlist some assistance from the people around you. I've found out that if you help others most of them will help you in your time of need. I was not always the first to start the chain of events but I did learn after leading a number of people in difficult situations.

One of my sailors had a medical issue with his wife in port. I called him in and told him to go home, help his family and let me know when he was able to get back to the ship. It was what we called "basket leave." It wasn't chargeable to his account. I was also able to send a number of enlisted men to officer training programs or to educational advancement schools. What goes around comes back to you eventually. I command advanced one petty officer to first class rank. He followed me to my next ship as my admin assistant (Quartermaster). At my next ship I had the honor of promoting this same petty officer to Chief Petty Officer (CPO). On that ship I walked by his office and heard him in a conversation with the Squadron Personnel Office. It went something like this, "Damnit, Commander Jarrett wants this done right now." After he got off the phone, I reminded him that I was Commander Jarrett. I did know that my reputation and his ability to get things done was enhanced by his brashness. I didn't reprimand him for using my name.

I was officer of the deck for the departure from port in New Hampshire on December 31st. It was a frigid watch and I was in an exposure suit on the bridge. It was easy to tell that it was really cold because the sea water was freezing on every exposed surface. By the time we dove the ship there were 3 inches of sea ice on every surface above water. On the way back in from the at sea period I was again the officer of the deck. We routinely take a good look on sonar for any contacts to ensure there are none above us in close proximity that could cause a collision. We also bring the ship slowly up to periscope depth while going around and around on the scope at a high elevation. You can generally see the surface from at least a 100 feet submerged. In the Bahamas that water is very clear and you can see it at 300 feet. As I brought the ship up, I couldn't see anything. It was totally black. So I brought the ship on up to periscope depth. I still couldn't see a thing. It was like I came up under a black plastic bag. I drove the ship up to the surface and turned on the side lights and stern light. I couldn't see the stern light a couple hundred feet away. When we got to the bridge, it was easy to figure out why we couldn't see anything. It was a blizzard and the snow was blinding.

We put up a Plexiglas windshield that stands up about 18 inches above the top of the submarine sail. It had two side windows that were held in place with metal pins through the hinges. The snow was coming down so hard that the top of the metal pins were generating static electricity. They were glowing eerily green in the dark. It's called St. Elmo's fire.

Coming out of shipyard the ship is rearmed with its strategic missiles. We pulled into Charleston Naval Weapons Station to Wharf Alpha and loaded two missiles for the Demonstration and Shakedown Operations (DASO). Because the ship was previously equipped with Poseidon missiles, we loaded them and trained and tested the system thoroughly. Then we proceeded to Port Canaveral to await orders to launch a missile down the East Coast test range. Nuclear submarines train continuously to ensure that we can do our job proficiently. There is more technology on a nuclear submarine that in the space station. We were ordered to the launch point in the Bahamas and then given a simulated launch message to launch the missile. We took the ship to hover depth and proceeded with the launch and everything went as planned.

I never did understand the next operation. After testing the Poseidon missile and completing the DASO launch, we were later directed to enter shipyard a second time and we upgraded our missile system to the new Trident I missile. So after the upgrade we proceeded again to Port Canaveral and executed a second DASO with the new missile system. Again, everything went as planned. The greatest difference between those two missiles is the range to targets. With the newer missiles we didn't have to go so far north in the Atlantic Ocean to get within range of our target packages. So that allowed us to have much more operating area and still cover our target packages.

Stealth port visit (You're not very stealthy when you're tied up next to a Soviet cruise ship.)

A bit later after a couple of patrols, we were granted a port visit in Ft. Lauderdale. That has to be to best port I've ever been in for a port visit. We always have two security guards topside who are armed with weapons. I was the duty officer and I toured topside to check on them and found a third guy there. He was acting kind of sheepishly standing up next to the submarine sail structure and had something behind his back. We had a continuous parade of boats come by checking us out while we were in port. This 425-foot black submarine generated a lot of curiosity. It was not uncommon for us to see 40-foot cigarette boats and other million dollar boats come by for a look at us. So I asked the sailor topside what he had behind his back. He slowly pulled out a piece of cardboard with the words "drop your tops" on it. I asked if he'd had any takers so far and he said, "Two in the boats and one on the pier." After you've been at sea for a couple of months I had to just admire his originality and let it go.

On another trip we were tasked to pull into port in the Bahamas. We noticed after we tied up that there was a cruise ship parked behind us on the same pier. It didn't look like a regular cruise ship like the Holland America Line or one of the Holiday Cruise ships that operate out of Charleston, South Carolina. For one thing its superstructure was covered with antennas like those used for intercepting radio signals. We discovered that it was also flying a red hammer and sickle Soviet flag. We always lower all of our antennas down into the sail in port anyway so it was funny to watch the cruise ship passengers come past our ship and pose for pictures with us in the background. My comment was, "They finally found one of us." We didn't have any negative interactions with any of them during the port visit.

When we pulled into port in the Bahamas the water alongside the pier was deep. The tugboat came alongside and got up close to the right location. But I really surprised the pilot when the ship moved sideways to the pier. Most people don't know that we have a 325-horse electric outboard on a shaft that we can lower beneath the ship and train 360 degrees. Submarines that I've been attached to were all single screw ships. Unlike the cruise ships and surface warships who mostly have at least two screws and some have side thrusters. They can maneuver more easily that we can because they can twist the ship by going forward on one screw and back down on the other at the same time. Also our screw is aft of the rudder and their screws are generally forward of the rudder. The only way we can steer the ship is by speed through the water.

In port was not always without its issues. (You train and train but accidents happen)

The topside watches were both armed with .45 caliber pistols. When they changed the watch and the new guys went to relieve the watch, they changed custody of the weapons topside. They had a five-gallon bucket full of sand and were taught to point their weapons in the bucket and clear the chamber of any rounds and then safely turnover the weapon. On one occasion we heard a loud noise topside and I went up to investigate. The topside watch had put his finger on the trigger while he was clearing the weapon and fired a .45 round. Thank goodness nobody was in the line of fire and no one was hurt. However, the fairing over the missile deck is thin steel about ½ inch thick. The pressure hull is about 3 ½ inches thick of much stronger Hy 80 steel. The problem was that that fairing is the cover for the main ballast tanks. We had six main ballast tanks and each held over a million gallons of water. To surface, we put air in those tanks from our 4500 psi air banks in what is called an emergency blow. The tanks have a rapid action popit valve on the top operated by 3000 pound hydraulics for rapid diving capability, but on the bottom they have louvered openings with a grate. We also have the capability to blow those tanks with our low pressure blower in a much slower fashion. The topside watch had fired a .45 round into one of the main ballast tanks. They are separated port and starboard in each tank. Air started escaping and the ship actually listed over to one side and the air leaked out that was keeping us afloat.

Deep Diving
(The sea is unforgiving at deep depths. Be prepared to deal with unexpected situations that can change your life.)

As the Main Propulsion Assistant (MPA) you are in charge of the mechanical systems in the engine room associated with the reactor and the steam systems for propulsion and electricity generation. We routinely did a deep dive coming off patrol to ensure the integrity of our sea water systems. On one of those deep dives I was engineering officer of the watch (EOOW) in the maneuvering space of the engine room.

I would routinely take a tour and inspect all the equipment at least once per watch. I was inspecting the Lithium Bromide (LiBr) air conditioning unit during one of those deep dives. The unit was enormous. It was rated as 110 tons of air conditioning capacity. Your home probably has about 3 tons of air conditioning. Some other factors are that this unit uses steam to create the cooling. I'll not try to explain that here, but if you buy me lunch we'll talk about it. It also is cooled with sea water injection. The unit normally operates at a 30-inch vacuum and has a gage on the front that probably measures about 18 inches across. It had a glass cover and was made of metal. As I was inspecting the LiBr air conditioning unit, we ruptured three sea water tubes in the unit. It immediately went from 30 inches of vacuum to over 500 pounds of pressure and blew the gage off the machine. If I'd been two feet to the left, I would have been decapitated. The gage was obliterated against the metal surge tank behind me. We isolated the flooding and proceeded to a shallow depth. No other equipment was damaged and nobody was hurt. My family and friends routinely kept me up in prayer while I was at sea. My favorite Psalm is 139. We call it the Submariner's Psalm:

> Whither shall I go from thy spirit? Or whither shall I flee from thy presence? If I ascend up into heaven, thou art there: if I make my bed in hell, behold, thou art there. If I take the wings of the morning, and dwell in the uttermost parts of the sea; even there shall thy hand lead me, and thy right hand shall hold me. (KJV)

While I was on the *James Monroe* I also studied nuclear engineering and took my "Engineer's exam." The ship had a data base of previous questions from exams but they were extensive and very comprehensive. It's not like you get to review the "real exam" questions. It's like you get to review the nuclear engineering text books. I don't know what the pass rate is for the exam, but it is extensive and long and has six sections such as nuclear physics, reactor controls, electrical engineering and power production, primary and secondary chemistry control and radiation control. You must pass every section independently and you must pass three oral interviews after that. You are given seven and a half hours to finish the exam. This is not a pop quiz. I took the exam and passed it with the result that I became qualified to serve as a department head on a nuclear ship. My next duty however as department head was not as Engineer but as Navigator and Operations Officer.

Submarine Officer Advanced Course (SOAC) (Learning to be a Department Head. Train your relief so when you move up you will have consistent knowledgeable support.)

Before going to my department head tour, I had to complete the Submarine Officers Advanced Course at New London, Connecticut. It was about six months long. Taking a chance, I decided that I didn't want to live in the Bachelor Officer Quarters for six months, so I found a house in Mystic, Connecticut and bought it. I also found a roommate from one of the junior classes. The house was in pretty sad shape. There were three layers of wallpaper on the living room walls. There were no doors on the cabinets in the kitchen. Upstairs the previous owners had pulled off the wallboard and installed insulation. They didn't bother to tape and mud the joints afterward. The upstairs was about 40 feet long with slanted roofs on both sides. There was a window on one end but nothing on the other end. It was a cave.

However, I'm pretty handy with a hammer and saw. So I installed a skylight on the dark end of the top floor. I also installed a bathroom in that area. I cleaned up and taped and mudded the wallboard and painted the area. It turned out really nice. Downstairs, I built some doors for all the kitchen cabinets and removed all the wallpaper and painted the rooms. The fireplace especially turned out really pretty. It got pretty tight on funds buying all the materials, so having a roommate really helped me to be able to still eat!

One memorable storm occurred while I was in New London. The weatherman had been predicting a blizzard for several days. So the Submarine School decided to not cancel classes until noon of the blizzard day. There was at least 6 inches of snow on the ground by the time they closed the school. I was driving a Toyota Celica back then and the ground clearance wasn't that great. I headed home to Mystic as soon as I was released from classes. I almost made it home. I was well within a couple of blocks of my home. Then I got stuck and couldn't make it any closer to the house. So I parked on the roadside and walked home. The next morning I went to find my car. Thank goodness I left the antenna up. It snowed about 21 inches. Fortunately, I was able to dig my car out before the snow plows destroyed it.

I sold the home after only 8 months and made a good profit. When I returned to Norfolk , Virginia to pick up my new submarine I was able to buy another home in Virginia Beach.

SSN at sea

Simuated target

4

CRUISE FROM HELL

Hell is not only a final resting place for the unsaved; it can also be a state of mind in times of trouble.)

I was detailed (assigned) to the USS *Baton Rouge* (SSN–689) in new construction as Navigator and Operations Officer after my tour on USS *James Monroe* (SSBN–622 Gold). The *Baton Rouge* was the second in the Los Angeles-class fast attack submarines. It was a different mission from the ballistic missile submarines that I had previously been operating on—much faster, more aggressive and a hunter killer mentality. The Los Angeles-class SSN is only 6000 tons versus the 8000 tons of my previous SSBNs; but had twice the horsepower. It could really push the water. At max speed at 500 feet down we would leave a four-foot wake on the surface and there is no boat. I remember coming into port on one occasion at night in Norfolk and we were going a pretty good clip on the surface and there were a number of small boats fishing off to our right with lights on them. They were rocking and rolling after we went by in Thimble Shoals Channel.

Fast attack submarines (SSNs) are given more freedom to make port visits than the Ballistic Missile Boats (SSBNs) to which I had previously been attached. We were ordered to pull into Halifax, Nova Scotia for a port visit. While we were in port the recreation committee organized a lobster party for the whole crew. It was a great event!

I remember one incident before we left for the Mediterranean in the harbor of New London, Connecticut. We were one of the first Los

Angeles-class submarines and had a towed sonar array before they had adapted them to be retrievable. The array was towed behind the ship on a cable over 1000 feet long. It was negatively buoyant, meaning that it would sink if the ship didn't have any forward speed to keep it off the bottom. We actually would bring a landing craft alongside with a tug keeping us moving forward while we locked the screw in place and they would fish the array out of the water just behind the ship and disconnect it from the ship and reel it in to a big reel on the small craft.

New London is not a new port and has some submerged wrecks on the bottom in the harbor. They are plotted on the nautical charts with the depth of the wreck annotated. We would do a race track in the harbor to keep the array off the bottom but we also knew how deep the catenary of the array was based on our speed. The captain was on the bridge and as navigator I recommended we turn to the left to avoid a wreck which was plotted at 187 feet deep which was shallower than our array on our present course. The captain disagreed and said, "I want to turn to the right." I repeated the request to turn left and stated that there was a wreck that we needed to avoid. He fiercely replied, "I want to turn to the right." So I tried one last time and stated, "The navigator does not concur, recommend a left turn. It is so logged in the ship's deck log." He turned right anyway and ran the array over the submerged wreck. In port he informed the squadron that it was probably a shark bite that ripped the array up. A million dollars later we got another array.

We were the first Los Angeles-class submarine to make a Mediterranean deployment so a lot of people wanted to see how we performed. Being on a new construction fast attack submarine was different from the slower patrols of the ballistic missile subs. We didn't just hide, we also chased. The ship was also quite a bit faster than my previous ships. I was navigator and operations officer and had two division officers working for me and a number of enlisted men in the navigation team and the radiomen.

On the way to the Mediterranean we were tasked to simulate an attack on a carrier battle group which was coming home from deployment to the Mediterranean. The carrier had seven surface ships out in front of them as a screen and all were active on their sonars. The SQS–26 and SQS–53 sonar systems put out about a megawatt with each pulse. We could hear them a 100 miles away. They were doing over 20 knots in formation and doing flight ops with planes taking off from the carrier. We attacked them right "down the gut" from the front. We had rung up maximum speed and the 60,000–horse power ship was flying. They must have thought we were noise in their sonar systems. We pulled up alongside the carrier and shot him from a close range. The Admiral was on the carrier and squadron refused to allow us to file the report. Thank goodness for periscope photography. We had pictures with cross hairs on the carrier and you could even see the planes taking off. Sometimes a picture is worth a thousand words!

The biggest issue that I had on *Baton Rouge* was not the operations nor the new technologies. It was simply the captain's violent temper. His normal way of talking to me was six inches from my face spitting and screaming. It was not just me even though I took the brunt of the abuse. He also fired both of my division officers and both of them left the Navy as a result. He actually fired me five times and rehired me six times. He also disqualified me as ship's duty officer and as Officer of the Deck (OOD) and requalified me for both positions. The problem was I kept better records than he did and it infuriated him.

After we pulled into port on one occasion I was scheduled to be the ship's duty officer. It's normal procedure to tie up to the pier and to take on shore power, then shut down the reactor and do maintenance on various ship's systems. On this occasion we had been out for a while and immediately when we hit the pier, the captain, the XO and most of the other officers and a good part of the crew left the ship on liberty. When the port facility brought over the four shore power cables to hook us up to pier power, one of them had a six inch hole burned in the insulation all the way to the copper conductors. Each cable carried 400 amps of power. We were steady state on minimum self-sustaining power and I would not allow them to use that cable. I called the captain's phone to let him know that the cable was not usable. I determined that because we might not have enough power to start the reactor back up with the remaining cables if we had to get underway in an emergency, we wouldn't shutdown. They promised to get us another cable quickly. It didn't happen. When the captain finally returned from liberty, he was furious and disqualified me from being duty officer for "making the reactor unsafe, because the watch standers had stood more than 6 hours of watch."

At one point he fired me as Navigator and we were getting ready to make a transit in the Mediterranean. He told me to navigate us through the Strait of Gibraltar. I reminded him that he had fired me the day before and the executive officer would have to do the navigation. There comes a point where you need to protect yourself. In the Mediterranean for five months we transited eight straits and logged 29,000 miles. We participated in many exercises and even participated in a big NATO exercise with 50 other ships. During that exercise we were where we were supposed to be and executed every task given for every one of them. Because my communications officer had been fired, I personally wrote every message that left the ship in addition to doing all the navigation and running all the operations. I also was one of three officers of the deck and therefore I was on watch six hours and off watch twelve hours continuously. Without any division officers, and running two departments and three divisions I also had 23 collateral duties including Secret information custodian, Top Secret information custodian, Special Compartmented Intelligence custodian, senior watch officer for all the other officers, and senior member of the examining board for all enlisted promotions. I simply couldn't get any sleep. When we came into the Mediterranean and I navigated through the Strait of Gibraltar, I'd been up for four days on six hours of sleep. The captain put me in port and starboard watches (six hours on watch and six hours off) so he could run engineering drills. I was wiped and couldn't sit down during watch or I would go to sleep. As a result, I stood up at the periscope stand the entire watch. While I was attached to the USS *Baton Rouge*, I was deployed out of area 78% of the time. When I was in port the rest of the time, I was in three section watch rotation. That means that I was on the ship 100% of the time on one of every three days.

The executive officer also informed me that I was to be taken to captain's mast (a legal proceeding). I had never heard of an officer being taken to mast. The XO said they wanted to do it in the Captain's stateroom to avoid me being embarrassed. I refused and said I wanted it in the crew's mess hall in front of the entire crew. We compromised and had it in the officer's mess in front of the officers. My assistant navigator, a chief petty officer, was also there. When the XO charged me, my Chief stood up and testified on my behalf. That took a lot of courage. All the charges were dropped.

To go or not to go? (When the going gets really tough, do you cut and run or stand and fight?)

We were in port in La Spezia, Italy for Christmas for five days and I took leave and went to Rome by train. I took all my belongings with me and wasn't sure if I would be back. After thinking about it for quite a while, I decided I could not let my Dad down and go Absent Without Leave (AWOL) or be an Unauthorized Absence (UA) as it is known in the Navy. During this entire time I had been calling my detailer (assignment officer) in Washington, DC. continuously. I called him 22 times in all. Finally, he sent me orders to submarine USS *Stonewall Jackson* (SSBN-634 Gold). The captain was Ron Urice, a Christian, who allowed me to do my job without harassment.

I knew that my fitness report from *Baton Rouge* was going to be trash, but as I said before ,I kept my own records. I submitted an eight-page rebuttal single spaced with dates, times and names to my fitness report. The *Baton Rouge* captain refused to sign it. So I appealed to the Commodore. I also submitted it to Senator Sam Nunn, who was my U.S. Senator from Georgia. Senator Nunn was on the Armed Forces Committee in the Senate. The Commodore ordered the *Baton Rouge* captain to sign the report. I not only made commander but also got selected to be the captain of USS *Daniel Boone* (SSBN–629 Blue). Wonders never cease.

Ship's patch, USS *Baton Rouge* (SSN–689)

USS *Stonewall Jackson*
(SSBN–634 Gold)

"The Old Navy"—Beards!

5

THE HEALING YEARS

The Lord sends times of peace and healing when we are at the end of our ropes.

Elaine Crouse and I were married in August of 1981. I was the Navigator on the USS *Stonewall Jackson* at the time. After we got engaged I went to sea for three months. Elaine's dad was an oral surgeon at the Medical University of South Carolina. Three hundred people were invited to our wedding. Elaine's mother asked Elaine, "What if he goes to sea and his head clears and he backs out of the wedding when he gets home?" The two mothers also got together and said they didn't want the beard in the wedding pictures. So when I got home I shaved it off. In all I was at sea for 50% of the time for the first ten years we were married. It took a special lady to stick it out during those deployments.

I've made a number of cruises in the Caribbean and the water there is very clear. Taking the submarine up to periscope depth is a routine evolution. In that clear water especially during the day time you can see the surface above you even down at 300 feet. On the way up we go around and around on the periscope at max elevation to ensure there is nothing above us. Sail boats are especially hazardous since they make almost no noise that our sonar can hear. On one of those periscope ascents, I was going around and around and suddenly a huge grey shape appeared. We have a standard casualty procedure code word, "emergency deep." Just before I was going to give that order, I noticed that the shape was looking at me. It was a dolphin hanging upside down looking into the periscope window!

Special Port Visit (You always need to know where you're going and what the channel looks like.)

While I was navigator on USS *Stonewall Jackson,* we received a message to pull into port in Tampa Bay. That may sound routine, but it was anything but that. We were operating in the Atlantic Ocean and Tampa Bay was in the Gulf of Mexico. Again that wasn't a big problem—we had a nuclear reactor and fuel for 25 years. I could not remember a nuclear submarine ever entering the Gulf of Mexico. One problem emerged really early after getting the message to execute the port visit. According to Navy procedures we carried navigation charts in accordance with a publication called N1. We were required to have those charts in hardcopy on board. Just one glitch, Tampa Bay was not listed on N1. I proceeded to determine how we could get a chart. It would be an embarrassment if we had to cancel because we couldn't navigate up the channel. We certainly didn't want to run aground trying to enter port for a recreational port visit. Unlike most patrols, we were not under communications blackout restrictions. So I contacted the U.S. Coast Guard. They probably had a good laugh about it but they agreed to send me a chart. Then the issue then became, how they were going to get me the chart in time for my navigation team to plot the entry safely? We concluded that they had helicopters and we were off the coast and in range. As a result, they helicoptered a chart out to the ship off the coast in exchange for 12 lobster tails and dropped the charts down to my team on the back deck and we got ready for the transit to the pier. I thought the price was reasonable!

There also was another issue. One of the surface ships had hit the pilings and knocked down part of the Sunshine Freeway the previous year. We had to transit that same strait to get to the pier. The wreckage had been cleared, but I have to say I did ask the pilot if he was the one who had piloted the surface ship into the bridge. He was not. Most people think that you pull into the harbor and tie up. Not in Tampa. It was a 33-mile transit up the bay to the pier that we tied up to. When I told my navigation team where we were tying up the word got out very quickly to the crew. We tied up to "Hooker Point".

I graduated from Stephens County High School in 1968. While I was in submarines my hometown newspaper, *The Toccoa Record,* published articles about my awards and my career pretty frequently. I know that because my Mom used to cut them out and send them to me. My high school asked me to come and speak at a student assembly and I gladly agreed. I took a bag with me to the speaking event and thought I'd have some fun with them. I stuck the bag under the podium from which I was speaking. I tried to encourage the students to believe in themselves and strive for higher things. At the end of the speech I pulled the bag out from under the podium and put on my football jacket from Stephens County High School. They loved it.

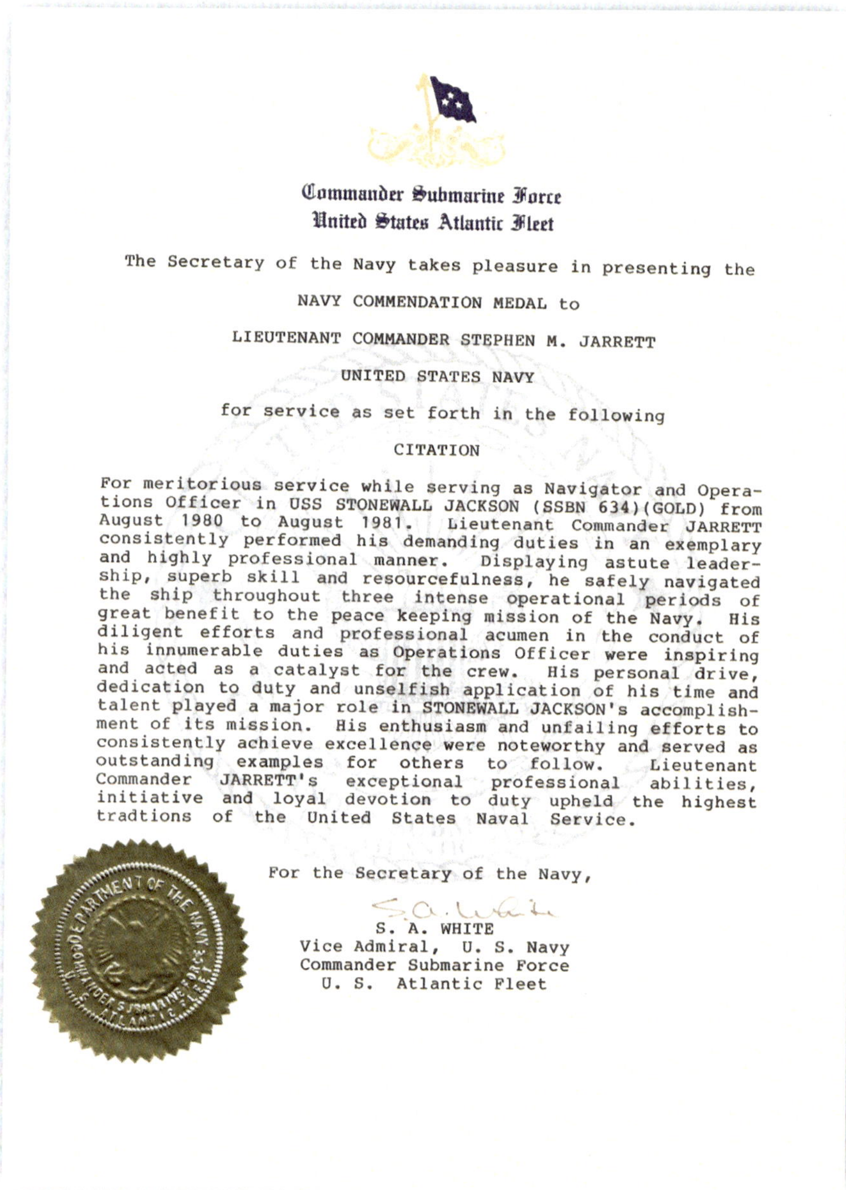

Commander Submarine Force
United States Atlantic Fleet

The Secretary of the Navy takes pleasure in presenting the

NAVY COMMENDATION MEDAL to

LIEUTENANT COMMANDER STEPHEN M. JARRETT

UNITED STATES NAVY

for service as set forth in the following

CITATION

For meritorious service while serving as Navigator and Operations Officer in USS STONEWALL JACKSON (SSBN 634)(GOLD) from August 1980 to August 1981. Lieutenant Commander JARRETT consistently performed his demanding duties in an exemplary and highly professional manner. Displaying astute leadership, superb skill and resourcefulness, he safely navigated the ship throughout three intense operational periods of great benefit to the peace keeping mission of the Navy. His diligent efforts and professional acumen in the conduct of his innumerable duties as Operations Officer were inspiring and acted as a catalyst for the crew. His personal drive, dedication to duty and unselfish application of his time and talent played a major role in STONEWALL JACKSON's accomplishment of its mission. His enthusiasm and unfailing efforts to consistently achieve excellence were noteworthy and served as outstanding examples for others to follow. Lieutenant Commander JARRETT's exceptional professional abilities, initiative and loyal devotion to duty upheld the highest tradtions of the United States Naval Service.

For the Secretary of the Navy,

S. A. WHITE
Vice Admiral, U. S. Navy
Commander Submarine Force
U. S. Atlantic Fleet

Recognition for service aboard USS *Stonewall Jackson* SSBN–634

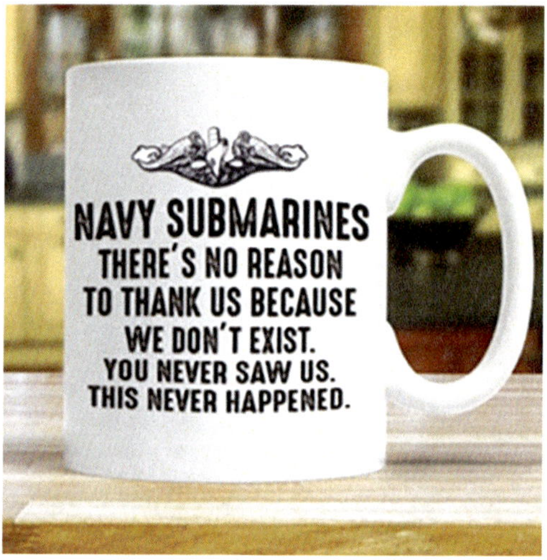

Without the sea there's no Navy;
without coffee, there's no sailor—
not that we were ever there anyway!

6

THE FLEET BALLISTIC MISSILE SUBMARINE TRAINING CENTER (FBMSTC)

It was good shore duty learning and training others to fight as professionals.

I chose to request a shore duty in Charleston after getting married. I was a tactics instructor at the Fleet Ballistic Missile Submarine Training Center (FBMSTC). I was tasked to teach ship crew how to shoot torpedoes in a computerized trainer. In the training center the ship's sonar team was in a separate room and all the systems worked for them. They could hear and track the contacts. Also they could hear the torpedoes when they were shot and the entire fire control team was live in the control center. Elaine said that I played video games all day. I guess that was basically accurate. When I got there they were running each scenario ad hoc. I didn't think that was acceptable or easy for my team so I started writing scenarios up on 5 x 8 cards with a picture of the setup and a track for the enemy contact to run. The operator then followed the script during the run unless I directed them to deviate. I also set up some rules. "If the crew being trained did something stupid that would alert the target like getting too close or making noise, or going too fast and cavitating the screw, I shot at them with an enemy torpedo." I was so accurate with my counter shots that my team made up a fake Order of Lenin medal and gave it to me when I left the center.

On a standard day of training we would start off with basic runs and I would pick the scenario cards out and give the staff one for each run. I had all the necessary setup criteria on the card and each was numbered. It might be a submerged target or a surface target. By the time I left the center I'd written about 120 scenarios. The training center in New London heard of my cards and requested them for their tactical trainer as well. When I left the center after a two-year tour, every submarine on the East Coast that was rated Above Average in torpedo warfare was one I had trained. Some of the torpedo settings in the SECRET manuals were ones I had requested and changed.

Some of the crews were easier to train than others and it greatly depended on the Captain of the ship. One crew that I trained had a captain that had a violent temper. I had a female petty officer acting as engineering on my team to answer bells for the simulation. He chewed her out so vociferously that she couldn't talk and I had to replace her during the training set. But "rules are rules" he kept doing unwise maneuvers during the runs. For the first week of his two weeks of training, I sunk him every run with a torpedo from the enemy ship. The second week was better and they improved a lot. After the second week, the captain marched directly into the office of the captain of the training center and I guessed that I was probably done and needed a new job. He told the captain that he was very mad during the first week, "but he'd learned more during his two week training session that he'd learned in the last ten years in our trainer." So I didn't get fired that week.

Elaine and I also took this shore duty as an opportunity to expand our family and our second son, Andrew, was born in 1983 at the Charleston Naval Hospital. He was a big boy and weighed 9 pounds 11 ounces at birth. His foot print was almost too big for the birth certificate!

USS *Von Steuben* (SSBN–632 Gold)

7

LET'S DO IT ALL AGAIN.

Going to sea again after shore duty as second in command you need to pass on what you've learned to the next generation.

I went back to sea as executive officer of USS *Von Steuben* after my tour at the Fleet Ballistic Missile Submarine Training Center. We were stationed out of Kings Bay, Georgia but the crews lived in Charleston, South Carolina so we were able to stay in our home there and be with our families while we trained in Charleston. Elaine got very good at driving from Charleston to Kings Bay also. When we deployed we'd relieve the Blue crew and take the ship in Kings Bay and they would come home to Charleston. We would do maintenance and training on the ship for 30 days in port except for a sea trial period and then depart on a 70 day patrol underway. The time on board worked out to be about a 100 day cycle. We were submerged for the entire at sea time usually unless we got really lucky and got a port visit. They were few and far between.

Ballistic missile patrols are usually very standardized and routine. The standard patrols were a three-day turnover of the crews, 30 days in refit and maintenance, a three day sea trial at the end of refit and a 70-day patrol. I've talked to some people who think we go to sea and sit on the bottom, but that is far from the truth. We actually never stop moving. Our primary mission is to remain undetected for the entire patrol. We don't tell even the good guys where we are. We do have a patrol area, but it is about 100,000 square miles and it also moves around. Why is that important? As the first line of defense for the nation, we must remain stealthy and safe from compromise. I've toured the land based ICBM silos and they have heavy doors and are buried under the ground. There is a fact that they don't take into account. Their location is known and it doesn't move. They are targetable by our enemies. A one megaton nuclear bomb digs a hole a half mile deep. Our stealth is our protection. They can't find us to target us. We constantly work on sound reduction. You almost have to run into us to find us. My ship alone had almost 10X all the bombs dropped in World War II. The Ohio-class SSBN has 30 times the destructive power of all bombs dropped in World War II.

As the executive officer (XO) of a submarine I had a number of duties that I had not done before in my previous jobs. First of all, you are responsible for backing up the captain in his decisions. That doesn't always mean that you agree with them. No one else on board can easily give the captain advice that maybe you might want to consider a different path on some leadership issue. That is all private. You are also in charge at the scene of any casualty, while the captain usually goes to the control room and makes sure the operational staff (Officer of the Deck, diving party and fire control parties) are heading the ship in a good direction for the particular casualty. I've had fires and flooding submerged. Sometimes the sea is against you and coming up to periscope depth to ventilate isn't possible. When the waves are 20 feet it's difficult to maintain the ship at the proper depth to ventilate smoke out of the compartments. If there is flooding, we obviously want to come shallow, but surfacing is not always possible. If propulsion is lost, there are other considerations. We always operate as a team. We train continuously to ensure the safe operation of all systems in casualty situations. Combat is a whole other realm of operations.

Change of Command

Missile Launch

Soviet AGI

8

COMMAND AT SEA

When you're in command or the top level manager, raise each member of your team to the next higher level. Their success is your success and legacy.

To qualify to take command of a nuclear ship you must pass the qualification exams given by Naval Reactors in Washington, DC. The Prospective Commanding Officers (PCO) are required to attend a 13-week training course led by the designers of the reactors. This is not your standard 9–5 course with weekends off. We generally worked about 80 hours a week and had a sectional exam every two weeks. Those exams were four hours each. I took copious notes and had 14 one-inch binders of notes at the end of the course.

Because I knew that I would be deploying immediately after taking command, Elaine and our boys closed up the house in Charleston and moved in with me in Crystal City (in Arlington, Virginia) into my Temporary Assigned Duty (TAD) apartment. Elaine got Metro passes and they toured all the museums and parks in Washington, DC for the summer. I worked and studied. Naval Reactors was six blocks away so I walked to class every day. We were up on the 7th or 8th floor of the apartment building and had a balcony. That's where we watched the 4th of July fireworks over the Washington Monument. The boys also watched for me to walk home from work in the afternoons. I could see their blonde heads bopping up and down on the balcony from several blocks away.

There were surface ship PCOs in our class as well as submariners. Unlike the sub guys, some of them had not had the junior officer experiences that we had and were trained to aviator or other perspectives. They had a hard time catching up. One of my classmates was a submarine officer from Charleston who was coming off shore duty as the nuclear training department head at the Fleet Ballistic Missile Training Center. His family did not move to DC during our school. He chose to drive home to Charleston frequently on the weekends. On one of the sectional exams, he didn't do as well as the instructors thought he should have done. He was given a one question reexam as a make-up exam. The grading was always subjective but generally fair. I guess he had not prepared well enough. Our training told us these criteria. If you know the answer, tell them the answer. If you don't know the straight up answer, using your knowledge of the question try to develop the answer. If you don't know either, tell them what you do know about the subject. Never leave the answer blank. He didn't do as well as they thought he should have done and they pulled his nuclear qualifications that day and kicked him out of the school. To say that the nuclear power program takes no prisoners is an understatement.

I had to wait a few months to get into my Prospective Commanding Officer (PCO) School so I was detailed to be the field representative for the development of the Advanced Capability Mk-48 torpedo. I was the Naval Sea Systems Command Field Representative for PMS 402 (the test office of the Program Executive Office of Submarines of NAVSEA Systems Command). I did a number of trips to the Bahamas to ride and observe the test launches of that new weapon. We did 65 launches testing the weapon. The submarine captains all knew me by that time and Elaine said I went to the Caribbean on vacation every two weeks. I do remember riding home by hitching a ride on a C-130 aircraft to get back in time for son Andrew's birthday party. There were six torpedoes in the back of the aircraft stacked two high and secured with chains. The aircraft was so loaded down that the pilot backed up to the end of the runway, hung the tail over the grass and gunned the engines. When he got to the end of the runway he pulled back hard on the stick and took a high angle and hoped he could get airborne. I was in a jump seat next to the torpedoes and I prayed for the chains to hold because they were under high tension with the 3600-lb weapons and vibrated violently.

After completing the thirteen-week nuclear power Prospective Commanding Officer (PCO) School at Naval Reactors in Crystal City in Washington, DC, I attended the PCO School for tactical training at the New London, Connecticut Submarine Officer school. They played war games and other things to teach tactics. I had previously been the tactical training officer for torpedo warfare at the Fleet Ballistic Missile Submarine training Center in Charleston. In one scenario they had assigned me to play the part of the commander of the Pacific Fleet and had the Soviet fleet led by their battleship, *Kirov,* sortie from the Kamchatka Peninsula to attack our fleet. It was scheduled to be a three-day game. However, it was a free fire hot war scenario and I executed a multi-submarine cruise missile attack coordinated from several different directions and overcame their defenses, sinking all the Soviet ships on day one. So they cancelled the other two days of the game.

I think the trainers also found out my background as the tactics instructor at the FBMSTC because they set me up on one of the torpedo approach scenarios. They caused an air leak in a forward ballast tank and the ship started to surface in the middle of the Soviet fleet. I brought the scope up and scanned as fast as I could. There were three Surface warships. I set up on the first one and executed a periscope approach. I called, "Bearing mark, angle on the bow mark and range mark. Set shoot." As soon as the torpedo was launched I set up on the second warship, called the bearing, angle on the bow and the range and said, "Set shoot." Then I did the same on the third warship. All three shots were hits so I sprinted to an escape. They brought a Soviet submarine active sonar from my baffle area so I did a "snap shot" over the shoulder and steered that weapon also to a hit on the submarine. They had had enough and completed the exercise.

I had my orders in hand to my command but they took a different turn. Elaine was the president of the Submariner's Officers Wives club of Charleston for Submarine Group Six. She came home from a luncheon meeting with Admiral Stan Bump and told me that I was going to USS *Daniel Boone* (SSBN–629 Blue). I showed her the written orders to the other boat. She was right, however, the *Boone* had run aground in Thimble Shoals Channel coming out of Norfolk, VA trying to maintain station on the outboard. That is a 325-horsepower electric motor on a 14-inch shaft that can be lowered and raised beneath the ship. They had knocked off the outboard. If they had retracted the shaft, they would have sunk the ship with a 14-inch hole in the bottom and no way to stop the flooding. The captain was summarily fired. When I got to the ship it was totally demoralized. They were sentenced to more time in shipyard to repair the damage and I had never seen a ship less prepared or ill trained. I was coming off of seven years of continuous sea duty and was very well versed in all systems aboard.

In Command of USS *Daniel Boone* (SSBN–629 Blue) (Sometimes changes come about for a reason that you don't understand. Go with them and do what the Lord has prepared you to do.)

My change of command was in Charleston and my father, mother, brother, sister, wife and kids were all there. Admiral Bill Owens, the Submarine Group Six Commander, spoke at the change of command. He later became the Vice Chairman of the Joint Chiefs of Staff. I also gave a short speech. I was also presented with my "command at sea" insignia which is a golden star. I asked my Dad to come to the podium and pin on my insignia. He got up and slowly walked to the podium and I saw this tough Marine from another generation of fighters, tear up as he pinned on the star. I think it was only time I ever saw my dad cry in 81 years. He told Mom that it was the greatest honor anyone had ever given him, but he definitely deserved it. He had stood by me through many trials of my life. My dad was always there.

The First Underway in Command (Don't assume that people know how to do their jobs. Pray that the Lord will always be there as your backup.)

When I took USS *Daniel Boone* to sea for the first time as captain, I was very concerned with the level of competence of the crew. This incident may explain that concern. We went out of Naval Submarine Base Kings Bay and would cruise on the surface until we got to the edge of the continental shelf. The water is shallow off the coast out to a distance of about 70 miles and then drops off precipitously from about 120 feet to over 1000 feet. We always wait until we clear that shelf before diving the 425 foot ship. The sea trials is two days with a turnaround for personnel transfer in the turning basin followed by another couple of days. I'd scheduled us to surface around midnight and transit on the surface to Kings Bay the next morning. I'd been awake for about 48 hours due to my concerns. I kept my submarine coveralls on but laid down in my bunk temporarily.

A few minutes before midnight I was awakened with a start almost as if someone had shaken me, but there was no one there. I knew something was wrong and I needed to take immediate action. I leapt up out of my bunk and sprinted the 50 feet to the periscope stand. Before I got to the conning tower I heard the Officer of the Deck giving orders to "make your depth 350 feet, all ahead full, come to course 278." I countermanded the orders running down the passageway. Whenever the captain gives an order to the helmsman, he automatically takes the Conn. We would have run aground on the continental shelf in about 15 minutes. We would probably have lost the ship with all hands. Prayers work and you shouldn't drive submarines if you don't believe in angels.

One of my best memories is when we had what is known as a "Tiger Cruise" and got to take family members on the ship from Charleston to Kings Bay underway for three days. Also Admiral Carr, the Commander of the Submarine Atlantic Fleet, rode us for that trip. I walked by the wardroom where the officers eat and saw my Dad from the hills of Georgia having a discussion with Admiral Carr over a cup of coffee. My Dad with only an 8th grade education raised in the country could carry on a lively conversation with the Admiral in charge of all the submarines in the Atlantic fleet. My son, David, also got to take that cruise with us.

During my initial few months on the ship I started to ask some questions. I asked the officers who was the last man to take the Nuclear Department Head qualification exam in DC. It had been over three years since anyone had even taken the exam. They could not remember the last guy to take it. I called the officers together and made it mandatory. My option was everyone takes the exam, your option is whether you want to pass or not. I tutored every man personally with my notes from the nuclear PCO training and pushed seven guys through the exam in three years. The written exam is seven and a half hours long with six parts and three oral interviews. You fail one section or oral and you fail the entire thing. You get two tries. If you don't pass the second time around, they remove your nuclear designator and you're done.

One of my junior officers did well on the exam that they offered him the billet as Engineer on the Navy miniature submarine, NR1. You have probably never heard of that submarine. It has a miniature nuclear reactor, wheels on the bottom and claws to grab and retrieve things. You probably heard of the B52 dropping a nuclear bomb off the coast of Spain by mistake. It was retrieved by NR1.

The second in command is the executive officer. I found out he had not finished his qualification for command. No other department head on board was qualified for command. I told him straight up that he had six months to qualify or he would be fired. The qualification for command is not easy but it is doable and is required for advancement. He finished with my pushing him to get done. When I left the Boone, there were four officers not counting me qualified for command. We were the lowest ranked ship of eight in the squadron when I arrived, within six months after I left we won the Omaha Trophy as the number one strategic nuclear asset in the United States, that included the strategic bombers and the land based missiles. We were the first ship to win that trophy.

I had a very good weapons officer and we worked tirelessly on the strategic team for missiles and the torpedo fire control teams. We had four nuclear weapons inspections including a no notice Nuclear Technical Proficiency Inspection (NTPI) with a team led by an Army colonel. When we got the announcement for that team coming aboard, I called all the cooks together and said I wanted the best food you have fixed for the team while they are on board. We pulled baked stuffed tenderloin and baked Alaska for dessert and I gave a standing order that the inspection team was not to run out of hot chocolate chip cookies when they were on board. This sounds like a strange order but I had an ace in the hole. I had determined early that everyone on board needed to be professional. I had called the cooks together and told them during off crew in port that they could come to the office and we could teach them the Navy cooking manuals or if they enrolled in Johnson and Wales Culinary College in Charleston and got their chef's license and showed me their grades and certificate, then I didn't want them in the office except to check in twice a week. We had five licensed chefs. I had a pastry chef, one that did ice carvings and some great cooks. I told the pastry chef that I wanted a huge platter of pastries on the wardroom table when the team arrived. On day three of the exam the head team member came to me and said, "Please tell them to stop bringing the cookies. I won't be able to make it out of the hatch." I determined if they were happy and eating they wouldn't be writing deficiencies. We got no grade in any area less than excellent.

We also had a Tactical Readiness Exam (TRE) as well. I had previously had an altercation with the deputy commander for the Squadron. He was chewing out my engineer in front of the crew during a previous visit and I had called him into my stateroom. We had a discussion and I instructed him that he was not to berate my officers in front of the crew. If he had a problem, he could come talk to me or he could relieve me of command because I was the captain. He was the head of the TRE team and when he came on board he told me when he got there that we were, "Below Average" and we would miss with some of our torpedo shots. We had loaded ten exercise weapons. I told him we didn't miss with torpedoes. So I shot the first four weapons myself and started to announce on the ship's 1MC announcing system, "We are one for one. We're two for two. We're three for three. We're four for four." Then I put my junior officers in charge of the last six weapons. I was of course looking over their shoulders and occasionally I'd say "shoot" when I determined that the solution from the sonar plots and the fire control team was correct. I continued announcing the hits on the 1MC. When we got to ten for ten, you could hear the engine room watch cheering three compartments away. Just to cement the effort, I steered two of the weapons around and got second hits so we actually got twelve hits for ten weapons. I guess I made my point so instead of giving us a "below average" he generously gave us an "Average" even though the fleet hit rate average at the time was only 50%. The primary comment from the inspection team was, "The Captain always solves the problem in his head before the fire control team has a chance to get the solution." I took that as a complement, after all I was the Captain but he listed it as a deficiency.

We were given short notice to pull into Charleston for preparation for a "Follow on Test," FOT, for the Trident I missile system. Our missiles were 70,000 pounds each, three stage solid fueled rockets with a range of over 6000 miles. So we pulled into port and the Naval Weapons Station and offloaded the nuclear weapons from 4 of our 16 missiles. Each missile carried 8 nuclear weapons. They installed telemetry head dummy weapons on those missiles. We were restricted from doing anything to the missiles except scheduled maintenance. We did disable the launch system for the remaining 12 missiles that carried nuclear weapons. We were then sent to sea to await the receipt of a release order message to fire those missiles down the East Coast test range. No observers were allowed on board during the test. We travelled to the Caribbean launch point and got to the area about midnight a couple of days later. I figured we'd probably get the message sometime the next day. I was wrong. We got the message very quickly and commenced hovering at launch depth and executed launch procedures.

The missiles are launched with a small rocket motor called a gas generator that fires down and vaporizes about 30 gallons of water under the missile. The missile is shot out of the launch tube like a spit ball. The gases and vaporized water blow it out of tube. When initial movement is detected the fiberglass cover over the missile is sliced up like peeling an orange with detonation cord. We shoot right through it. The missile tube is pressurized with nitrogen to the same pressure as water pressure at launch depth so the missile has holes in all the missile access doors to relieve the pressure on the way to the surface. The missile actually breathes out all the way to the surface. If those holes weren't there, it would blow the doors off the missile on the way up. The missile rocket motor doesn't ignite until the missile receives a broach signal when it reaches the surface. We always launch submerged at hover depth. If the solid fuel rocket motor were to fire in the missile tube, it would burn the ship in half. When you are the captain and you give "permission to launch" knowing that twelve of your missiles have real nuclear weapons on board, and you feel the boat lurch from the missile away there is always a gut feeling and a prayer, "Lord I hope we did everything right." South of the equator they filmed the reentry of the warheads and it immediately reminded me of the passage in Mark 13:24–25: "But in those days, after that tribulation, the sun will be darkened, and the moon will not give its light, and the stars will be falling from heaven, and the powers in the heavens will be shaken." The reentry bodies look exactly like shooting stars and everything will be shaken when the nuclear bombs explode.

We also routinely had Operational Reactor Safeguards Exams (ORSE). We ran drills and trained our personnel all the time to ensure they could safely operate the reactor and fight casualties if necessary. We got ready for one of those exams and when the ORSE team came on board, I was familiar with the senior member, a Navy Captain. He was my former captain of USS Baton Rouge who had done everything in his power to kick me out of the submarine force. We ran the drills and reviewed all of our training records and other issues. I thought we did a pretty good job for a submarine that had run aground several years before and got delayed in the shipyard an extra year. It didn't matter to him how we did, he gave us a "Below Average" anyway. I guess I should have spent more time reading the "How to win friends and Influence people book."

Naval Submarine Base Kings Bay (It is 17,000 acres of wilderness on the Georgia border with Florida— an old Army depot with wild boars, snakes and lots of deer.)

My first introduction to Kings Bay, Georgia was very early in the development of the Submarine Base. Jimmy Carter had determined that the old Army depot would be a great way to funnel money into the depressed economy of South Georgia. The submarine base was just north of the St. Mary's River Channel separating South Georgia from North Florida. Ft. Clinch guarded the south shore of the channel entrance. It was an old abandoned fort from pre-Civil War times. Fernandina Beach, Florida and Ft. Clinch National Park and camp ground were right next to the park. There was also a breakwater around the entrance to the channel with huge rocks on both sides of the entrance.

In the early days the base was pretty rustic. The officer's club was an old ranch-style brick house sitting out in the live oak trees. We occasionally went over there to watch TV during the refit period while we were getting the ship ready to go on patrol. The inside of the "O" Club was classic animal house. The furniture was an old couch with the stuffing coming out and some old chairs. The bar was a refrigerator stocked with beer and soda and a paper cup inscribed with "put money here." We stopped going to the club at night after they killed a seven foot timber rattler in the yard. A picture of that timber rattlesnake did make it to the new officer's club when it was built.

The Kings Bay submarine base had a lot of paved trails that we jogged on to stay in shape and to de-stress during the month of upkeep. We frequently saw herds of whitetail deer on the base and our Commodore really had a blast hunting wild boar on the base with some South Georgia guides. On one of my jogs I met a snake sprawled across the paved trail. The trail was about 6–7 feet wide and you really didn't want to jog off the trails. The snake was off the pavement on both sides and since I couldn't see his head or tail I decided that "discretion was the better part of valor" and retraced my tracks in the opposite direction.

As captain of the USS *Daniel Boone* (SSBN–629 Blue), we were in Kings Bay when the first Ohio-class subs came to the submarine base. Because Daniel Boone, the man, was quite a pioneer, we had a replica of "Tick licker," his musket, mounted in a case in the wardroom on the ship. Because I was the captain and we wanted to generate higher morale on the ship, I wore a coonskin hat with scrambled eggs on the front from the bridge when we drove in and out of port. My mother-in-law had given me that coonskin cap at my change of command. The anti-war protesters amassed a group on Ft. Clinch for the arrival of the USS *Tennessee* SSBN–734 (the first Ohio-class submarine) into Kings Bay. We were on sea trials which were broken into two two-day segments with a personnel transfer in the turning basin at Ft. Clinch in between.

With a three knot cross current at the rocks of the harbor entrance, I brought the ship in with a full bell and our 14-foot screw was kicking up quite a rooster tail. One of the protesters on the beach pointed at us and my coonskin hat and made the assumption that this must be the USS *Tennessee.* Out came the horde of protesters carrying six coffins and wearing yellow radiation suits. There were horse policemen to keep order and we were laughing from the bridge. When we got even with them I put on the brakes with a back full and shot water fifty feet in the air to stop the ship in the turning basin. They were really confused on the beach and began to congratulate each other on turning around the USS *Tennessee.* The tug came alongside and we executed the personnel transfer and I kicked the ship back to a full bell to get speed on before we hit the current at the jetties with another fifty foot 30,000 horsepower rooster tail. The protesters were so busy celebrating that when the USS Tennessee arrived three hours later, they were nowhere to be found.

Soviet Intelligence Ship Interactions (Most people think we are alone but the enemy is never far away.)

Being a submarine captain and operating out of a secure base like Kings Bay, Georgia you don't expect to have many interactions with Soviets close to home. That ended up not being the case for me in command. The "normal" Russian intelligence ship off the coast was an older Okean-class ship of about 120 feet in length.

They would play cat and mouse with us when we were going in and out of port. They routinely stayed just outside the territorial limits at 3 miles from land. On one occasion we were leaving port for sea trials and the Okean AGI was waiting for us. The seas were running about ten feet that day and it was reasonably rough for small ships. With my ship being 425 feet long and drawing 32 feet draft on the surface, it wasn't a big deal for us. The AGI began his run to catch us and I pushed him directly into the waves. Every time he went over a wave he'd fall into the trough and the waves would break over his bridge. In inland waters we are required by the "inland rules of the road" to copy continuously on the bridge to bridge radio telephone. After a few minutes he had apparently had enough and he transmitted on his bridge to bridge radio telephone, "Captain Jarrett, Dosvedenya." That's "until we meet again" in Russian. So much for security. They knew not only which ship we were but also who was the captain.

On a later excursion they weren't so accommodating. This time a newer and much larger AGI was off the coast. It was a Balzam-class who had two huge radar domes topside. He was also about 344 feet long, about twice the size of the Okean.

We picked him up at some distance away and he came roaring in from our port side. We were racing to the dive point. The continental shelf extends out to about 70 miles off the Georgia coast and due to our size and draft we can't dive until we clear the shelf. The water goes from a depth of about 120 feet to 1000 feet in a matter of a couple of miles. We were moving fast but the Russian was faster than we were. I'd already cleared the bridge of all personnel and items and had the ship rigged for diving. As we closed in on the deep water diving point the Russian cut across my bow in violation of the rules of the road. We reached the shelf as he tried to cut us off, so I pulled the plug and gave the order to dive with me on the bridge. I dropped down the open hatch and dogged it behind me. I ordered the diving officer to level off at a reasonable depth and we went under the Russian.

Hurricane Hugo (Some storms in our lives are bigger than anything we've ever experienced. Prayer and fellowship are what gets us through those hard times.)

In September 1989, USS *Daniel Boone* was on patrol in the Atlantic Ocean off the coast of Africa. We were covering targets and maintained our stealth with the best traditions of the silent service. As we executed our mission we tracked a storm as it was born off the coast of Africa. It made its way west and gained strength day by day. It seemed to have its eye on the east coast and our homeport of Charleston, South Carolina. After tracking it for almost a month the monster Category 5 storm, now named HUGO, hit McClellanville, South Carolina just north of Charleston.

It downed all three Submarine Group Six transmission towers. I put the ship at periscope depth and copied all the news we could get. We started receiving Radio Free Africa that was broadcasting reports of dozens killed and thousands homeless in Charleston. Still, there was no report from our commander about the families. Hugo hit on September 21st and I immediately began to hold daily prayer services in the crew's mess. We sang hymns and read Scripture. More and more crew members started showing up for the services. We started having thirty five to forty men at each service. At one point I had a senior Chief Petty Officer in my stateroom crying in worry about his family. On October 9th, eighteen days after the hurricane hit our home port we finally received a simple message from Submarine Group Six that all the families were accounted for and no one was injured. We had major damage to six homes. Before deployment I had appointed two ombudsmen who were also the wives of crew members to assist the 80 wives and families. They had executed a reverse phone tree and had accountability on all dependents on the 24th of September. We had done our job, we had protected America, but they had forgotten about us. My wife had gone to the Group Six Commander and read him the riot act. She got the wives and families checked on and taken care of and sent men from the opposite crew to patch roofs and help them get to safe shelters.

I had seventeen years of sea duty in my submarine career. That's more than most submariners. I completed 18 three-month patrols on ballistic missile boats and a five-month patrol to the Mediterranean on USS *Baton Rouge* (SSN–689). I went back at one point after being Navigator on two different submarines and estimated how many miles

I had submerged. When I got up to 350,000 miles I stopped counting. Some of my time was in the Bahamas and the Caribbean but most of it was in the North Atlantic. With the older A-3 Polaris missiles we had to go further north due to range restrictions. So I've operated north of the Greenland, Iceland, and United Kingdom Gap (GIUK Gap). One thing is pretty consistent about the North Atlantic in winter time. It's rough. My last patrol in USS *Daniel Boone* we were in 20-foot seas or higher for more than a month. We saw 50-foot seas on that run. Most people think that submarines just submerge and get out of the weather. That's true for some things but when it's really rough and the water is deep, it's just not that easy. We were taking 30-degree rolls at 500 feet down.

I've also operated north of the Arctic Circle. That's about 60 degrees northern latitude. One thing about that is that the water gets really cold. You don't need much air conditioning when the sea water injection temperature is 31 degrees or below. I have on occasion put salt in the bilges to keep the fresh water drains from freezing.

After one of the northern patrols we were tasked to pull into Halifax, Nova Scotia for a port visit. This was a surprise for us as a ballistic missile sub. The commander of the submarines in the Atlantic Fleet (COMSUBLANT) ran a wargame scenario and it was sent to us. The scenario was that we experienced an antiwar protest on the pier while in port and there was a mob group marching down the pier on which we were docked. My response was "don't let them cross the brow, even if we had to fire our weapons." They recommended that we push the brow into the water and have the topside watches evacuate even if it meant that they would have to jump over the side into the water. They said my actions would cause an international incident. I replied, "If my topside watches evacuate their posts due to the threat, I'll shoot them myself." We had a full load of nuclear weapons and sixteen solid fueled intercontinental missiles under the deck. A shaped charge could penetrate our hull and ignite a missile motor resulting in the ignition of other missiles and effectively burning the ship in half with the loss of all hands.

The response went all the way to the Commander in Chief Atlantic Fleet (CINCLANTFLT). He agreed with me not COMSUBLANT. I don't remember getting any response from COMSUBLANT after that exchange. Every warship and US military unit always has the right of self-defense.

My high school and Stephens County officials got together and organized a "Stephens County Hall of Fame." They elected three people each year to induct into the group. I was elected on the first ballot. While I was in command of *Daniel Boone,* I invited a number of friends from my hometown to come down to Kings Bay for a tour during one of my in port periods. I arranged for them to have access to get on base and gave them a tour of the ship. We also scheduled them for a meal in the wardroom with my officers. They had a great time and talked about it for many years.

USS *City of Corpus Christi* (SSN–705)

United States of America

Commonwealth of Kentucky
County of Bell
City of Middlesboro
TO ALL TO WHOM THESE PRESENT SHALL COME,

Greeting:

KNOW YE THAT COMMANDER S.M. JARRETT AND CREW OF USS DANIEL BOONE
IS COMMISSIONED AN

Admiral
IN THE

Old Yellow Creek Navy

I hereby confer this honor with all rights, privileges and responsibilities thereunto appertaining.

The said Commissioned Admiral to defend Old Yellow Creek, its environments, and all its tributaries.

In testimony whereof, I have caused these letters to be made patent.

Done at Middlesboro the Third *day of* October

in the year of our Lord one thousand nine hundred and Eighty-Eight

and in the Sixtieth *year of the Old Yellow Creek Navy.*

BY THE COMMODORE

FIRST MATE

Honorary Admiral, Old Yellow Creek Navy

Luce Hall, U.S. Naval War College, Newport, Rhode Island

"Victory through Sea Power"
U.S. Naval War College
motto and logo

9

U.S. NAVAL WAR COLLEGE

It was a time of studying, strengthening, and recuperation; we all need that after stressful situations.

The detailer didn't want to send me to the Naval War College. When I talked to her about it she said that she would really have to crack some eggs to get me into the class. I bought a small porcelain bird's nest with eggs in it and sent it to her to get in. The main reason was that Group Six had rated me low in the group of commanders of their submarines and as a result, at the end of my tour at the Navy War College, I was passed over for promotion to the rank of captain. I had been taking correspondence courses from the Navy War College at sea and had finished two thirds of the course before I was sent there. So I asked to be an "advanced research associate" for one trimester. My topic got approved and I worked independently for a trimester. My topic was, "Application of Submarine Technology and Experience to the Space Program." I was able to get access to the international space station blueprints, casualty procedures and atmosphere control specifications. That was the good part. The bad part was that they were all wrong. The "jet jockeys" of the space program didn't have a clue how to fight casualties in a closed space nor were they using the right limits for atmosphere contaminants. Submarines have been operating in closed spaces since the 1950s in nuclear submarines like the USS *Nautilus* (SSN–571) and have extensive experience there. Some of their decisions were to be expected due to inexperience in that environment, but some were almost funny if they had not been so serious.

Submarine or a Space Station?
(I've talked to many veterans and when they get out of the armed forces they need to evaluate what they really know not what jobs they had in the service)

Space station engineers were really concerned about particle impingement of a pea-sized meteorite travelling at a high speed punching a hole in the 7-cm aluminum skin of the space station with a result being that all the air would gush out and the astronauts would suffocate. I told them to give him a roll of duct tape, tear off a piece and put it over the hole. They were aghast until I pointed out that it was only 14 lbs of pressure and duct tape would easily hold that. Submarines at deep depth, however, couldn't plug holes with duct tape. At about 1000 feet submerged the pressure is over 500 psi. It's a totally different issue.

The atmosphere limits were also wrong from a submariner's viewpoint. I pointed out that half of the oxygen limit they proposed was above the submarine limit due to fire prevention. They eventually changed the limit. They also didn't track trace contaminants like we did. For example, we greatly limit freon levels. Their documentation actually said dicholorodiflora methane would drive the Trace Contaminant Analyzer (TCA) into saturation and they would not be able to sample the atmosphere. I asked if they knew the common name for that methane. They didn't. It is commonly called Freon-12 which is what they use in the refrigeration system to keep their food safely stored. The TCA runs at about 600 degrees to break down the air into its components to sample. At 600 degrees it turns freon into hydroflouric acid, which will etch glass. If a flame is present about 2000 degrees, it forms phosgene gas, which was used in World War I to kill soldiers in the trenches in Europe.

Their limit for carbon dioxide was also set at 3 ppm which was about half of the limit we set in submarines. I told them that it was way too restrictive. The argument that I got was there would be severe physiological effects on the astronauts with the higher level. So I sent the space station people in Houston a one-foot stack of medical reports from the Submarine Medical Research Laboratory to support the higher limit. Houston called me and said, "Commander Jarrett we agree. We'll change the limit." Why was this important? They spent millions of dollars developing systems to get the CO_2 level down to their limit. They could have used our CO_2 removal systems right off the shelf.

There were a number of other atmosphere issues that I provided to NASA's Johnson Space Center and to the National Space Council. Submarines are closer to space stations than any other options. Aircraft travel in the atmosphere but for very short periods of time. They also don't usually fight major casualties and have to maintain livable atmospheric conditions for long periods of time. We measure patrols in months, they measure them in hours.

Another area of concern was radiation control. My research discovered that in 1972 during a three-day period there was a major solar flare. We don't normally associate that with radiation but instead do know that it can affect microwave transmission and other issues due to the blast of ionized particles impinging our satellites and the atmosphere. There are also significant effects like the Aurora Borealis or northern lights. Our atmosphere protects us. In space it does not. During the three-day event the astronauts would have gotten 450 REM of ionizing radiation. That is a 50% mortality rate. The space program simply changed the limits for the astronauts by a factor of 10 and did nothing else. I received a phone call from one of the Space Shuttle captains about this. So I designed a radiation shield for the habitation module to be used as a storm shelter in case of major radiation events. The shield was segmented so it could be carried up in small parts and bolted together. We only needed to shield one side of the habitation module of the space station to give them a storm shelter since it is stationary in orbit to always point the solar arrays toward the sun which was also the source of the majority of the radiation.

The Space Station documents cited concerns about circadian rhythm specifically that involves day and night changes. Since the space station is in relatively low earth orbit we can occasionally see it pass overhead when the moon reflects off the unit. As a result, the astronauts see days and nights in a matter of a few hours instead of like we do on the surface of the earth, every 24 hours. When submarines check out on patrol, we frequently chop to Greenwich Mean Time (GMT). The submarines pass over multiple time zones on a transit east or west and the operational orders are linked to a time that doesn't change. To avoid confusion and to make sure we stay in our assigned area of operations, we use a standard time. So what that means is that when we come to periscope depth and the ship's time is 1200 noon it may be dark outside. The Quartermaster of the watch and the navigation team keep track of sunrise and sunset so the conning area can be rigged for red at least 30 minutes before we try to ascend to periscope depth. Also the Officer of the Deck usually wears an eye patch over one eye so he is night adapted in case we have to go to periscope depth unexpectedly. Another aspect is that we normally run a three section watch bill. You are on watch for 6 hours and off for 12 hours. During your time off you sleep, train and do your maintenance. About one third of the crew of 165 is on watch all the time. What that means is that we normally operate on an 18-hour day. Also we have a meal every six hours including at midnight. That enables the oncoming watch to eat before they go on watch. I have to admit that I wore a 24-hour Ironman watch at sea. That way I wouldn't be surprised going to dinner at 6:00 and finding out it was breakfast!

I also worked with an Israeli company to design a wearable belt to protect the astronauts from radiation. Radiation doesn't affect all parts of the body the same. The limits for extremities such as hands and feet are much higher than for internal body parts. The parts most affected by radiation that are of concern are the blood producing areas. One primary area is the horn of the pelvis. If we protect this area, the astronaut can be exposed to much higher levels and recover. Because the astronauts are in a zero gravity environment, weight is not an issue. So we designed a belt with lead in it to shield these body parts from the ionizing radiation. It was very heavy but in space it was weightless.

The fire casualty procedure they were using was highly automated. They sensed fire or electric arc and automatically shot Carbon Dioxide at the source. I casually asked, "Where is the astronaut in the space station going to go? You just filled the compartment with CO_2 and he's going to die." They had not considered that. So they said, "He has an air pack." I asked, "How long does it last?" They replied, "10 minutes." So, I said, "Ok, he will die in 10 minutes." The air pack masks also covers only the mouth and nose. Ours covers the eyes also, because seeing in a smoke filled compartment greatly aids in damage control. Submarine masks are also air fed from a major air bank and I personally have spent over 8 hours in masks during casualties at sea when we could not ventilate the ship. Another major option is to simply deenergize the electrical equipment to put out most fires. I also asked if they used smokeless cable in their electrical systems. That is the cable that doesn't yield cyanide when it burns like the cable they were using. I gave them the specification for smokeless cable and a source for it from the shipyard. I provided the Emergency Air Breathing masks to the space program and showed them how to put air manifolds in the station powered by their repressurization air bank to provide long term survivability to the occupants.

Having been the Electrical Officer on a submarine I also queried the Space Station designers about "selective tripping breakers." That's a design that the breaker closest to the fault trips first and the rest of the circuitry is protected. It's standard on submarines and an easy way to put out fires without shooting CO_2 or fire extinguishers in a closed space. Most fires in submarines, probably more than 80% are electrical and can be put out that way.

Training Our Allies

While at the Naval War College I was detailed to be one of the sponsors for the international students. Most people would be surprised to find out that only about half of the students are U.S. officers. They also have international officers there and other service officers from Army, Air Force, Coast Guard, and Marine Corp as well as some other government agencies. I sponsored the senior Venezuelan commander, the senior Turkish commander, and a junior officer from Chad.

José was from Venezuela and arrived with his wife and three kids. It's pretty warm in his home country and nobody even owned a coat when they arrived. I took them to Burlington Coat Factory and everybody got one. He called me and said his mother-in-law was also going to come with them. A few days later he called again and said his nephew was also coming. I looked around and found a house for rent for them to say in that belonged to another officer who was temporarily in California at a training command. They were great friends and we had some good times together. They also came through Georgia after the school and Jose's wife's brother painted a picture of my home place in Georgia that hangs in my bedroom today.

Because we had little boys, we were involved with the Boy Scouts. When the summer class graduated the students all left. I was in a March to March class because we were the sponsors for the international students. The Scout leaders brought a box of all the Scout records and stuff to me and said: You take the Scoutmaster position or the troop folds." So I got trained and we started recruiting new scouts. Only five were left. Elaine became the Cub Scout den leader and recruited 35 new Cub Scouts. I picked three assistant Scoutmasters. Two were Marine majors and one was a hydrofoil captain out of Key West. One of my Marines had done the "60-day sleeping in a snow cave test" for the Marines to test some new cold weather equipment. His son and my son became great buddies. We went from potentially folding to 19 scouts. At the Scout competition for Pokanoket District my Marines had trained our Scouts to the highest level. We won 8 of the 10 competing events. I had my brother's old Scout manual and it taught you how to do a "bean hole bake" for the Scoutmasters. I knew we were in when the judges came back for seconds. We were selected as the Pokanoket District Troop of the year.

I had been assigned to the team to select the "President's Award" winner for the previous class that graduated in June because I was in the class that didn't graduate until the next March. One factor about that is that I learned what the team used as criteria to determine who would be selected. It says "academic, extracurricular and community" achievements. As I mentioned above, I had taken the Scoutmaster role because there was no one else to do it. I had a lot of help and some highly qualified people helping and we were very successful. I also volunteered to teach a leadership class to the Naval Justice School lawyers who had very little at sea experience. Our family was heavily involved in a local church and I had even repaired the façade of my apartment in the senior officer housing. I guess it just goes to show you that after ten years of continuous sea duty you don't feel like just sitting around sipping coffee. It may not have been fair but I won the award anyway.

The same week that I was selected to win the President's Award as the honor graduate of the senior class at the Naval War College, I was passed over for promotion to the rank of captain (06).

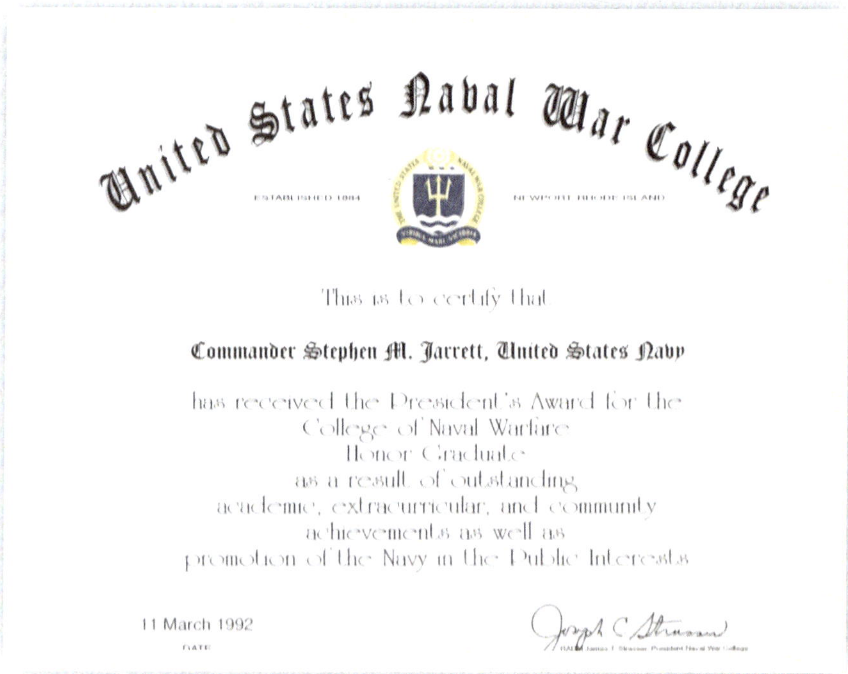
United States Naval War College

ESTABLISHED 1884 NEWPORT RHODE ISLAND

This is to certify that

Commander Stephen M. Jarrett, United States Navy

has received the President's Award for the
College of Naval Warfare
Honor Graduate
as a result of outstanding
academic, extracurricular, and community
achievements as well as
promotion of the Navy in the Public Interests

11 March 1992
DATE

President's Honor Graduate,
U.S. Naval War College

United States Naval War College

1884

Be it known that the President of the Naval War College by virtue of the authority vested in him by the Congress of the United States of America and upon recommendation of the faculty does hereby confer upon

Stephen M. Jarrett

the degree of

Master of Arts

in

National Security and Strategic Studies

in recognition of fulfillment of the requirements for that degree with all the honors, rights and privileges pertaining thereto.

In Testimony Whereof signatures as authorized are hereunto affixed, and the seal of the College is attached at Newport, Rhode Island, on this eleventh day of March in the year of our Lord one thousand nine hundred and ninety-two and of the College the one hundred and seventh.

Dean of Academics

President

U.S. Naval War College Diploma

Order of
the Rabbit

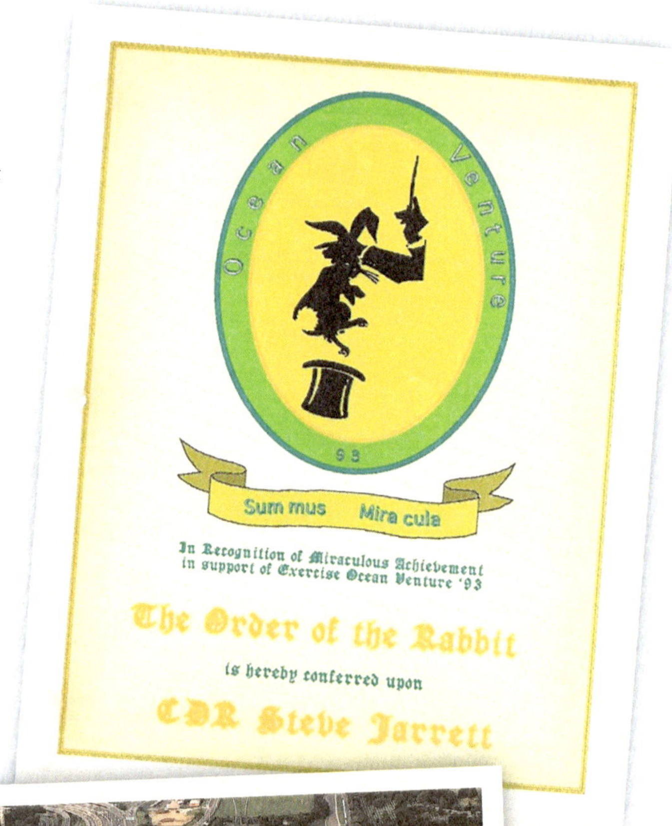

The Pentagon—"The Puzzle Palace"

10

THE PENTAGON

*Regardless of who you work for,
do your job as unto to Lord.*

After the Naval War College I accepted a position at the Pentagon on Vice Admiral Jerry Tuttle's staff. I was N60C, the Flagship and Joint exercise coordinator for command, control, communications, computers and Intelligence (C4I) systems for the entire Navy. I was also the Assistant for Space. We were having difficulties on major exercises and deployments of battle groups because one ship couldn't exchange data with the other ships due to non-compatible systems. I came up with "battle group books." When we had a pending deployment, I got a list of command and control and communications systems from each ship and compared them. These went into the battle books for each battle group. If a ship needed a specific upgrade, I petitioned the Assistant Secretary of the Navy for C4I for the funds and sent the upgrades with my technical representatives to put them in. I remember briefing Assistant Secretary of the Navy (Research, Development, and Acquisiton) Gerald O. Cann sitting at a table next to him. I flipped through the slides in the book for each ship and when we got to the end of the brief, he asked, "How much do you need?" I replied about $20M. He said OK. To learn the impact of these books is to understand that if a ship in the screen for the battle group picked up an incoming cruise missile attack it was imperative that they be able to electronically transmit the sensor data to the other ships of the screen to ensure that they could also take action to attack the incoming weapons if necessary. There isn't time for a phone call or a message with vague contact reports.

I was also the chairman of the design committee for the C4I suite for the flagship for the Mediterranean fleet. I chaired the committee and we designed the suite for the flagship. I also flew to Japan during that time to review another flagship upgrade.

After Admiral Tuttle and his deputy Admiral Jordan got to know me I got other assignments and duties. One I brought upon myself. Admiral Tuttle always carried a steno pad and wrote down reminders for himself for the things he assigned his staff to do with dates for getting them done. At staff meetings he would review these assignments. He had six captains as his staff over the departments. Admiral Jordan would get blindsided frequently because he didn't have any knowledge of all the assignments for the department heads. So I went to him and said, "I can fix this. I'll attend all the staff meetings and take notes." I made a simple Excel chart and listed all the assignments for the department heads with the dates due. I provided that to Admiral Jordan and he was totally informed whenever Admiral Tuttle asked him about them. After a couple of months the department heads started coming to me to check on their assignments. I'd frequently get, "could we adjust that date a little bit?" In affect they were all working for me instead of the other way around.

Admiral Tuttle also would ask me about assignments. My tech reps were stationed worldwide and reported in when they needed something. We had some Electronic Countermeasure systems on surface ships in the Far East off the Korean Peninsula that were having some problems. My reps had notified me and we were in the process of fixing them. Admiral Tuttle got a call from Vice Admiral Jerry Unruh, the area commander of that force, and he came and asked me what the status was of the systems. We had fixed the ship he asked about three days before and my tech team was on the way to fix the other four squadron ships that had the same problem. Admiral Tuttle didn't ask me about fixing systems much after that and he assumed I'd be on top of the technical issues.

The Pentagon has a good fitness center in which to work out and do physical exercise to keep in shape. Many days at my job there, I'd put my gym clothes on and jog during lunch time. My usual route was from the Pentagon down and around the Washington Monument and back at about a distance of 4 miles. That was before many of my knee issues later on. Also while we were living in Annandale just outside the beltway I joined a five-person carpool to get to my job every morning. I was driving a GMC Jimmy with a 6.2 liter diesel engine with four wheeled drive. So anytime there was snow or ice or even heavy rain I was nominated to drive that day. It's amazing in the DC traffic the little cars make a path when a rumbling diesel Jimmy is trying to get to work on time. It reminded me of the parting of the waters of the Red Sea for the Israelites.

We had purchased a home in Annandale, Virginia outside the beltway. It was not a large house but it did need some work. Elaine went to work on the kitchen and started peeling off layers of wallpaper that had mildew underneath. I started working on the basement. There was a fireplace there and I decided a little upgrade would make a lot of difference. I lined the front of the fireplace with rose colored marble tile and it turned out really good. There was a problem with the house overall that we discovered after a time. The house appeared to be slipping down the hill toward the backyard. The basement concrete floor was several inches out of being level. I leveled it with concrete, ten thousand pounds of concrete to be exact. I mixed it in a big wheelbarrow and poured it myself. We stopped parking our car in the attached garage as well since the slab going into the garage developed a two-inch gap of being level with the garage floor. We also reworked the front porch and entrance way to the house and I built some nice brick fan steps. It always seemed like we left houses better than we found them as we moved during my Navy career.

While I was at the Pentagon a newly-promoted captain was sent to be my boss. She had very limited operational experience and didn't know much about the systems or ships. Her at sea experience amounted to three years on a training carrier. I had a number of yellow stickies above my desk at the pentagon and each one of them represented a reminder to get back to a person on a technical issue in the fleet. She came to my desk and told me to take down all the sticky notes. My desk was on an inner ring of the fifth floor of the Pentagon. It was not a high rent district. I tracked the crack across the window on the inner court rooftop next to me with a magic marker. I remember giving one brief about a pending deployment of a battle group to the Mediterranean. She insisted on giving the brief but I had compiled and written the whole thing. We gave the brief to Admiral Jordan. At the end of her presentation, Admiral Jordan turned to me and asked, "Steve is this all right?" I replied, "Yes Admiral," and he funded the upgrades.

I don't remember exactly who presented me with "The Order of the Rabbit" award, but as best as I can remember it wasn't anyone from the Pentagon. It was from one of the operational commanders. I frequently pushed technology to the fleet that they didn't expect to happen so that they could do their jobs better. I tried to stay on top of any issues that would impede their success on any operations. I was the Flagship and Joint exercise coordinator for all command and control and communications systems for the CNO's office and Admiral Tuttle gave me a lot of leeway to make things happen. That is frequently the sign of a superior leader. When you make your staff successful they will frequently make you successful too.

When the time came for my second look at promotion, I had asked admirals that I had worked for to write letters of recommendation to the board president on my behalf. I had twenty-three stars on letters to the board. One came from my former Group Six Commander, Admiral William Owens, who later became the Vice Chairman of the Joint Chiefs of Staff. It didn't make any difference and I was turned down a second time so I retired from the Navy at the Pentagon in October 1993 after

21 years of service. My four years at the Naval Academy didn't count in that service time.

My bride calls this room the "I love me room." I guess that is ok. I have a number of awards, plaques and memorability that won't even fit on the walls. It is ok it reminds me of where I've been and where I'd like to go.

Shadow Box

Arctic Circle Certificate

11

ADVANCED TECHNOLOGY DEVELOPMENT, ROCKWELL

Never make decisions on major life issues out of an attitude of fear.

Admiral Tuttle was good friends with industry leaders and he recommended me to Jack Cosgrove, the CEO of Rockwell Collins. They hired me and I worked for Rockwell as a senior engineer in their Crystal City facility. After a few months they moved me to Cedar Rapids, Iowa. That was a cultural and environmental earthquake. I admit that I was afraid of not being able to pay the bills. The Bible says again and again, "be not afraid". In fact according to Dr. David Jeremiah who we listen to on the radio every morning it is the most frequent command given by the Lord. My life verse is Joshua 1:9, "Be strong and courageous, be not afraid nor be dismayed. Don't you know I'll be with you wherever you go?" Sometimes life gets in the way of good sense. I should have listened to my bride.

At Rockwell we were coming up on the year 2000 and many of the computer experts were forecasting doom and gloom. They expected that systems would not work at all after the roll over to the 2000 year. At Rockwell I was appointed as the "Y2K Coordinator." Nice title, but I felt like that was all a smoke screen to have someone to blame if things went downhill fast. Being a good naval officer, I took it anyway and ran with it. Rockwell Collins made major airline navigation and communications systems for 300 airlines. Many foreign airline companies used our systems as well as the US companies. We also had systems on a number of foreign military units. I looked and there were no standards for what "Y2K ready" for a system meant. So I wrote a standard. The first step was,"if the system doesn't know what year it is and it's not in the program, well, it is Y2k ready." We had 770,000 active products and four foreign company subsidiaries. They had tested nothing. I was designated as the only company person who could sign for Y2K readiness of any systems. The command structure came to a head when one of the vice presidents came to me with the contract from Boeing, our major customer, and said that I needed to sign that our systems were Y2K ready. I simply asked, "What have you tested?" The answer was "nothing." My answer was,"You don't test it, I don't sign it." After shutting down five contracts, the word got out really fast. I enlisted 150 engineers to test systems. My test criteria was upgraded some but most of the systems fit under,"too dumb to know the date." So that part was easy.

I went to the customers and asked for lists of their systems so we could verify their readiness. I eventually got over 1200 customer faxes of the lists of the customer systems. They listed not only our systems but our competitor's systems as well. We had products still active with the Turkish Air Force that were over 20 years old and still working. We found some interesting things out through the testing. Our airline navigation systems would work fine until the January 1st rollover, then all the programmed way points for the navigation system would disappear. In effect we would have had 8500 aircraft in flight that would have been lost. There was even an article in the *Readers Digest* that suggested that airline planes would crash due to Y2K errors. I reminded our engineers and customers that one could look out the window and fly the plane. As we tested the many systems we logged them into databases and I put up an online site for customers to log in and check the status of their systems. I was invited to Singapore to participate in the Y2K brief for 50 Asian airlines sponsored by Airbus. We briefed in a large amphitheater.

The Airbus representative briefed first and the question came from one of the airlines, "Is Airbus warranting their seven types of planes against any Y2K failures?" I thought the representative was going to back off the stage. I briefed after him. I projected my laptop on the screen behind me and did a live product search on line to show the customers that we had the most common 35,000 products in the database and they could check those easily. If they sent us a list of products, we would verify them and get them the results. We got millions of hits on our database during the first month it was in operation.

As the Year 2000 time zone rolled across the landscape worldwide, I received reports back from my technology representatives around the globe by email and phone. The Chief Executive Officer of Rockwell came in and asked me how it was going and I was able to give him updated reports every hour as my representatives reported in to me.

Earning Another Degree (I refused to let $35,000 of GI Bill benefits expire.)

When I had been hired by the CEO of Rockwell Collins, he had signed an agreement that they would pay 100% of tuition for advanced degrees. I told them I wanted to earn a doctorate. They replied that they wanted me to get a master's degree. What they didn't know is that I already had taken advantage of the Naval War College (NWC) program and had a Master of Arts in National Security and Strategic Studies from the NWC and had done a second master's in management with Salve Regina University in Newport, Rhode Island at the same time. After sending a request through the CEO of Rockwell three times they relented and agreed to pay for my doctorate. Then I made a deal with them. I'd use my GI bill until it expired, but they would pay for travel and lodging and it wouldn't count as vacation However, every paper that I wrote would be double routed to them. I wrote 25 research papers of about 25 pages each. My topic for my dissertation was, "Factors Affecting the Adoption of E-business in the Aerospace Industry." My dissertation is 165 pages and was published by Nova Southeastern University, Wayne Huizenga Graduate School of Business and Entrepreneurship. I was also designated by Rockwell as the Principal e-Services Manager. Maybe I'm a serial entrepreneur. I also enlisted 35 more students for the doctoral programs for Nova Southeastern University and became the NSU representative for the Midwest. They would fly the professors in and we would conduct courses locally for some of the requirements. The university also agreed to pay me $800 per month for setting up and running the program.

A Miracle in South Carolina

"We" make our plans but the Lord may have other things in mind. I believe that sometimes He laughs when he sees what we are planning.

I guess it's funny to start a South Carolina story in Iowa but that's where this one starts. After seven years in Iowa working for Rockwell Collins we had a dreadful winter in 2001. In the month of February the temperature never got above 0 degrees. I'd never seen weather that cold for that long. Elaine's comment was that it was "too cold for human habitation". While we were in Cedar Rapids we saw one time where the temperature went down to –29 degrees. We ran gas logs in the house frequently and it was common to have ice on the windows, on the inside of the house.

With Andrew accepted to Virginia Tech for his freshman year of college and Paul was getting ready to start high school. The boys and Elaine came to me and said, "Dad we're moving; are you coming?" So I put out resumes and started looking for a job back east. The Navy Base in Charleston had closed down and that didn't seem like a viable option. The market wasn't great but I ended up with a couple of job offers in DC. One was as the deputy Chief Knowledge Officer for a major defense contractor and the other was with a small consulting firm in DC. At

Rockwell I had been on the Gartner Knowledge Management Council and the National Software Consortium.

We put our home up for sale in Cedar Rapids, Iowa. With Elaine's master gardener's skills the outside of the home was a beautiful garden. I'd built a wooden fence around the backyard with a Charleston Fan gate and we'd expanded the deck and put in an overhead lattice work so it was beautiful. Inside I'd refurbished the kitchen with new Swanstone countertops, an island and new appliances the year before. We'd also finished up the basement and installed another bath, gas logs and since I couldn't get Goodwill to take the old counter tops and appliances, I'd put a full kitchen in the basement. The basement was basically unfinished when we bought the home. The floor was concrete and there were two metal poles supporting the center of the house. It was a great big open area. My kids used to roller skate down there. The outside walls were poured concrete about 8 inches thick. On the outside they were made to look like bricks. I put 1 ½ inch Styrofoam insulation all the way around the basement wall. Inside that I put 2 x 4 studs and put fiberglass roll insulation between the studs. We then sheet rocked the basement including the ceiling. I rented a lift that enabled me to hold a sheet of sheetrock in place against the ceiling studs to attach it with sheetrock nails. It took 76 sheets of sheetrock to finish the basement. I replaced the basement windows with better ones and was able to load the sheetrock into the basement through the window opening. Elaine did most of the finishing of the mudding of the joints after I put the joint tape over them. She's an artist.

We had our own tornado shelter. With the thick walls and insulation you could see the wind blowing outside the windows but you could not hear it at all. Also with the addition of the gas log fireplace in the basement and the extra insulation, we could almost heat the house with just the logs even when it was below zero outside. The church youth group also liked it because not only did it have a TV but also a kitchen down there. It was perfect for fellowship meetings for our kids youth group.

Because I was already an electrical engineer from the U.S. Naval Academy, I determined that house wiring couldn't be too tough. I got information on the electrical code from the city and studied up for a while. Then I went to the city and took the code exam and passed. I put eight new circuits in the basement for the addition and the new second kitchen including the range and oven. It was all inspected and passed. I got one discrepancy on an outlet in a main floor bathroom that came with the house. It was one that I didn't wire.

Being the Y2K lead for Rockwell, I took the effort to build a big pantry with shelves in the basement. We completely stocked it with emergency food just in case it was not available after the rollover of the century.

We talked to a realtor and told her what price we wanted and she balked at the number. After she looked at the house, she agreed. A woman came to look at the home with her realtor and took a walk around, sat down at the kitchen table and wrote a contract for full price, without even talking to her husband. We sold the house in four days. With the date of the home closing approaching Elaine and I went to DC for a house hunting trip. The problem was that two weeks after the closing both job offers fell through. I felt the Lord wanted us to move out of Iowa but I didn't have real good directions from there. In DC, Elaine and I looked several days at the available homes. The prices were astronomical. Then came the fact that I didn't have a job and to get a loan without a job was problematic at best and almost impossible. It was a test of faith. With it raining that afternoon, Elaine and I drove by our old house in Annandale. Close to the house we saw some kids at a church having an unsuccessful car wash in the rain. We pulled in and had them wash our suburban. We talked to the leaders while the kids washed the car and after they finished they surrounded us and prayed for our situation.

Elaine and I went back to the Ft. Belvoir Bachelor Officer's Quarters where we were staying and talked about what we wanted to do. At one point in the conversation that evening, I told Elaine that because we didn't have a job any longer in DC, we could go anywhere. I asked her where she wanted to go. She simply said, "I'd like to go home to Charleston." We received a call that evening from our realtor in Charleston and she informed us that the renters in our home in Charleston were three months behind in the rent and she was taking action to evict them from our house. We had a place to live. Still no job or a good school for Paul, but we had a home again.

We'd been working with Thomas Jefferson School of Science and Technology in Fairfax County Virginia which was one of the leading high schools in the country and had preregistered Paul. He is a special student and was two years ahead of his peers in math in Iowa. We'd gotten teacher recommendations and all of his transcripts forwarded to Virginia and were ready to enroll him as soon as we found a place to live. We'd been told by the realtor that the renters were fighting eviction and had requested a jury trial. I've never understood that with them three months behind in the rent, so we went directly from Virginia to Charleston for the trial. In Charleston I decided to check for schools for Paul on my father-in-law's computer. We found that there was an Academic Magnet School so we made an appointment and went over to visit the school. It was on the old Navy Base that had closed about ten years before and was surrounded by crumbling buildings from the base but the school was impressive. Ms. Dobson was a great counselor and she told us that the selections for the coming year would be made on Friday of that same week. It was already Tuesday and we scrambled to get the application together. Mom and I called the Thomas Jefferson School of Science and Technology in Fairfax County in Virginia and got them to fax the entire package down to Academic Magnet. We were elated when they selected him on Friday.

Now we had a school for Paul and a home if we could get the renters evicted but we still didn't have a job. I'd applied for a job at the Space and Naval Warfare Systems Center in Charleston but had been told that there were no jobs available. I guess God had other plans. A week later I got a call from SPAWAR to come in for an interview. The Chief Scientist had resigned after being there only eight months. His wife couldn't deal with the summer heat. My wife loved it. I went in for a 30-minute interview and left Elaine in the car. After a three-hour interview and a tour of the building, I finally found her in the lobby. I came back from Iowa for another interview but they still couldn't hire me due to the requirement to advertise the job in the Federal BizOps.

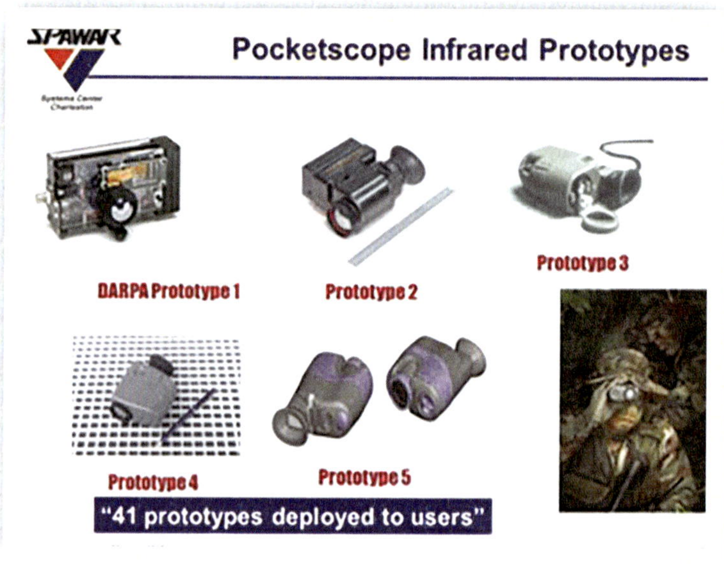

We developed prototypes of needed
and cost-efficient equipment.

12

CHIEF TECHNOLOGY OFFICER, SPACE AND NAVAL WARFARE SYSTEMS COMMAND

Use your ideas from your experiences to see innovations in a different light.

You may surprise yourself by applying what you know to new and different situations.

With SPAWAR needing someone to take over for the leaving Chief Scientist duties and administer the Defense Advanced Research Project Agency (DARPA) contracts, I incorporated myself as Dolphin and Eagle Consulting, Inc. and took the job as an interim fill. The Lord had provided a job, a home, and a school for Paul. We did have a huge setback with Andrew at Virginia Tech. We had applied for a Naval ROTC scholarship for him and he had been accepted. The issue was that the DoD Medical Exam Review Board (MERB) found the word "asthma" in his record when he was 8 years old. He'd had issues with allergies and we had taken him to a specialist. He'd overcome them and had been on the varsity soccer team at high school for three years. I'm sure he could have outrun all the members of the DoD MERB but they labeled him as "physically disqualified" and removed his scholarship. Elaine and I prayed about it and decided that Andrew would stay at Virginia Tech. We scraped together the out of state tuition. It was

$200 per month higher than our house payment. Andrew did great. He was one of only three midshipmen to pass the first physical fitness test. He did 83 pushups in two minutes. The NROTC Captain worked with me to get his application approved for a waiver for the asthma disqualification and we scheduled a methacholine challenge test at the hospital. He passed it and we were able to get the waiver and the scholarship for the last four years for this five-year engineering program. The Lord had provided again for our family.

SPAWAR Challenges

At SPAWAR I was kind of an anomaly. I had an operational background and approached issues and customer challenges from that viewpoint instead of the bureaucratic civilian way. When the troops needed a capability, I went to the labs and found them a solution. I'd put it in rapid prototyping and have them do most of the testing. I guess it worked because for the first six years of the ten that I was at SPAWAR, I paid my own salary and my staff salaries from the equipment that I sold. It was over $30 million. The Infrared Pocket Scope was a great example. DARPA spent $12 Million making two prototypes in Plexiglas boxes. Then they gave me the project to "transition" without any funds at all. I immediately saw the potential for a small infrared detector with 50 thousandths of a degree sensitivity. Up until our development, it took a cryogenically cooled sensor with liquid nitrogen to get that sensitivity. We did it with a 12-ounce unit on two AA batteries. We were working with the Raytheon Commercial Infrared Company out of Plano, Texas. My friend, Frank, was the program manager for Raytheon and we talked frequently. He was also retired military. I pushed them hard to get an operational prototype that I could market.

Three times they came to me and wanted a MILSPEC for the packaging of the detector. Finally, I told them, "Go to Walmart and get a sportsman flashlight. Gut it and put your electronics in the case. If I give you a MILSPEC the unit will cost $4000. I want it under $1000 per unit." When the prototypes arrived they even had the rubber ribs on the outside like the Walmart flashlights and they were priced at $995.

I shopped the prototypes to my military customers. Everyone has seen the night vision units on the helmets of the soldiers deployed. However, that unit is a starlight system. It basically intensifies light. In caves and inside buildings in Baghdad that we have knocked out the electricity, there is no light to intensify. Basically, you couldn't see any better than the bad guys. I had briefed the lieutenant colonel in charge of technology at the Army Rapid Equipping Force at Ft. Belvoir outside of DC. I got an urgent call from him and he simply asked, "Dr. Jarrett, how many of those pocket Infrared units do you have and how fast can you get them here?" I called Frank up in Plano. I said Frank, "Make them." He responded. "Can you get us on contract?" I went to work in Charleston and wrote a sole source justification. Then I went to contracts and worked with them to get an urgent contract together. It normally takes months to get a government contract approved. We had the contract finished and the justification for "combat." We put Raytheon on a $10 million sole source contract in 48 hours. I called Frank and told him I was coming to Texas with the contract.

When I arrived in Plano they arranged a tour of the factory for me. When I stepped into the factory, I got a standing ovation. They wanted to help the troops and I'd allowed them to do it. They made 70 units in 48 hours and 295 units in 23 days. They were shipped directly from Plano, Texas to Kuwait and married up with the 101st airborne. They went into Iraq with the first wave of troops. Later I got a call from Bagdad airport from a major in the Army Fifth Corps. You could hear gunfire in the background. The Major said, "Dr Jarrett, these pocket scopes are the bomb. Can we get some more?" In total we made and shipped over 3000 units.

Another project was a "microfluidics chip" that my friend, Dr. Yitzhak Rosen, a cardiologist at Johns Hopkins, designed and tested for the U.S. Airforce. You placed a drop of blood on the chip and read it with an optical reader. It would then tell you the blood type. It was quite an innovation. Being a submariner I asked the question, "What else could we dope the chip with to test for something else?" We worked with the director of the Hollings Marine Lab on James Island, Geoff Scott. They had an issue with contamination of the oyster beds in the harbor and coastal waters. Any time they had a pollution causing event such as a release of sewage or anything else including flooding due to a hurricane, they had to test the oysters for Vibrio vilnifungus bacteria (flesh eating bacteria) before any commercial fishing was allowed. They would ride around in a small boat in the harbor, take a sample, pack it in ice and try to determine its location and three days later they would have a result from the lab. Our system could take the sample and test it on the boat immediately.

We also did another development and worked with the Hollings Marine Lab to test it. At least that was the plan. About this time, the USS Cole got hit by a terrorist attack with an explosive device in a small boat. Seventeen sailors were killed. After analyzing the scenario, we determined that a warship in port had no protection from a swimmer attack other than turning the screw backwards or going active on the sonar system. In that case a French diver next door might be affected and quiver to the surface. So I found a system with a company out of Washington state called Biosonics. They had a portable sonar system that could be draped over the side of the ship and would give us visibility of a diver in water as shallow as 3 feet and even among the pilings of the pier out to 350 meters. I negotiated with the director of the marine lab to test the unit on their NOAA pier in Charleston Harbor. It was an underwater transducer connected to a laptop on the pier for the readout of the underwater picture. The Biosonics CEO had agreed to provide over $100,000 of equipment for the test free of charge. I had a meeting with the legal officer at SPAWAR for the second time and explained to him the test criteria and the equipment and the concurrence with the director of the Hollings Marine Laboratory. They were happy to let us use the NOAA pier because they had been running around the harbor looking for dolphins which they had a requirement to count. If we could count divers, we could also count dolphins in the harbor. During the legal meeting the Lawyer said there is no way we can do that test, "We might burn down the pier and we would be responsible." I admit I got a little upset. Ok a lot upset. I slapped the table and said, "You have to be kidding me. Well not exactly those words but close." We had a solution to prevent the terrorist's attacks on our ships in foreign ports, and we were afraid that we'd burn down a pier with an underwater sensor. He stood up and stomped out of the room and filed criminal charges against me for threatening him. David, one of my friends at SPAWAR, called me aside and said, "I have a friend that you should meet." He was a lawyer named Andy Savage. One Savage letter to SPAWAR and the charges went away. I never even saw the letter.

At SPAWAR I finished my doctorate in Business Administration with a concentration in Information Technology Management. I wrote pretty extensively. One of my concepts was the development of an Advanced Technology Transition and Innovation Center (ATTIC). My staff and I did extensive technology searches with the labs and small businesses. We pulled in various technologies that they had developed and didn't really know what to do with. One example was a trip I took to Georgia Tech. They set up briefs for me on 36 technology developments in two days. It was a fire hose. I was also on the program team for the Federal Laboratory Consortium. So we had access to the federal labs as well. The issue was that the lab developers didn't have any operational experience and couldn't see the applications like we could. I was employed by the Special Forces Command in Tampa, Florida for three years as a "technology scout." They paid for my time and gave me capability needs and I found technology solutions and provided rapid prototyping of the solutions. ATTIC was evaluated as one of the top five innovations during the Iraqi war by the Assistant Secretary of Defense. It was interesting to find out that even the University of South Carolina, who is not considered a huge player in research, had over 500 patents on technology that were available for licensing on their website. Research funding develops technology, but there is a big gap from the lab to the commercialization and fielding of these technologies.

With the Iraqi War going full speed, I got a request for help from Tampa to field a Psychological Warfare unit mounted on a UAV. This was not a small UAV. It was launched from the bed of a pickup truck. We were transmitting radio signals from the UAV and I reminded them that that was a very low tech area so we probably needed to drop radios to the ground before so they had some way to receive the radio. They proceeded to fly the UAV and launched it from the truck. When it got up to altitude they fired up the high powered transmitter. It knocked out the avionics of the UAV and it went into a hard right turn and crashed when it ran out of gas. So much for their first effort.

I looked for some commercial off-the-shelf solution that could be easily fielded. At a conference for radio broadcasters, I found a number of options. Yes we could transmit to a UAV but also they had programming stations that were in trailers or even an 18 wheeler trailer. They were frequently used by commercial radio stations to broadcast from sporting events. I called up Tampa and asked if they wanted a small UAV version or a bigger one. Sometimes you have to look in other disciplines to find a technology development that will fit your current needs. One thing that I learned by experience was that "what you name a development frequently limits where it will be deployed and developed." If you develop a system for use in an aircraft it is difficult to get it to transition over to a ground vehicle.

We previously discussed the pocket infrared scope that was developed with DARPA. I took that prototype to a dentist's office. If you look in a person's mouth who has any kind of infection you can easily see it because it causes inflammation that is hotter than surrounding tissues. I could stand in an inner room at my home and count the studs in an exterior wall due to the differential temperature. If you stood outside the home and looked at the roof you could easily see if any areas of the roof were losing heat due to lack of insulation. Materials are a difficult thing to transition but two that I got from Georgia Tech were an easy thought process. One was silicon carbide and the other was boron carbide. If you are not a chemist or a materials engineer you probably don't know much about these materials. They are both extremely hard but also extremely light weight. They were perfect for light weight body armor inserts for our troops in combat.

Also at SPAWAR I was designated as a technology transition agent for six DARPA projects. The DARPA program managers would pay my expenses to attend their meetings with their clients wherever the meetings were held. I have a very operational background and many of the developers were very academic. They were very well versed in their technologies but didn't have a clue what to use them for commercially. One example was the Polymorphous Computing Architecture (PCA) program. That's a fancy name for computers with multiple processors. Putting the hardware together was the easy part, but "how do you program the multiprocessor computer?" is a whole different subject. MIT actually put together a supercomputer with 32 processors during this DARPA program. I helped them develop the capability to program it. That program was called the Polymorphous Computing Architecture (PCA) program. I have a cap with that on the front and no one has ever been able to guess what PCA stands for yet.

I also did transition for the Advanced Cognitive Information Processing (ACIP) DARPA program. With a lot in the news right now about Artificial Intelligence, that program was before it's time. We also had a small business contact that developed some interesting UAV technology. We wanted to test it at the Navy Base but they had restrictions on flying UAVs there. So I contacted the Citadel and we flew them in the football stadium for the Citadel football team. Sometimes you have to make sure that the developers don't get over zealous. On one occasion one of my UAV developers had constructed a small UAV with a miniature 12-gauge shotgun attached. The unit had some sophisticated sensors also that included facial recognition software cameras. Seal team 6 came to Charleston to see some of our developments and the UAV developer wanted to demonstrate the unit to them. This was an anti-terrorist development. I could just see the headlines, "Charleston test gets off course killing Seal team members with armed UAV." I told them we'd provide video of the tests but no live demonstration.

Seal Team 6 was located out of Dam Neck, Virginia and they were responsible for taking down the Somali pirates that captured the merchant vessel (*Maersk Alabama*) that Tom Hanks made the movie about. What the movie didn't show was that three days before the take down, my team delivered twelve technologies to the team in Dam Neck.

During the Iraq War we were having multiple attacks by Improvised Explosive Devices (IED). I was on the Navy counter IED team for many years. One of the issues was that the IEDs were being triggered by terrorists with cell phones. They would hide away from where the explosives were placed and wait for troops or vehicles to come close enough to destroy and then send a signal from the cell phone to destroy them. I found some technology to jam that cell phone signal in Israel but encountered a problem when we wanted to test it out to see if it would be effective. Persistence has never been one of my weak points. There were laws in the United States that prevented us from testing that technology. So we looked for some other options. There is frequently a second or third requirement that would need a similar technology to what we want in the field of combat. Take for example a big church would like for people to be responsible and turn off their cell phones during services so they don't interrupt the service. Also a number of other large gatherings of people would like to not have people on their phones during meetings. With the jamming system being limited in range and easily controlled, we tested it in a Cathedral outside the U.S. with very good results. We used it to prevent the killing of our soldiers in the field.

Harvard Senior Executive Fellows Program

I never found out how the Navy got connected with the Harvard Senior Executive Fellows program, but SPAWAR was looking for someone to go to the Harvard month-long course at the Kennedy School of Government and nobody else wanted to go. They were paying for the course and all of my expenses so I volunteered. Other potential attendees thought a month away from home was a huge time. I've made 18 three-month deployments on submarines and one five-month deployment. One month to me was a piece of cake.

When I got to Harvard it wasn't quite what I expected. I don't remember exactly how many people were in my class. It was about 30 or so from a number of different government groups. There were even a couple of people in our class from government intelligence organizations. The Iraqi conflict was in full swing and one professor in particular was really upset about it. He continually bad mouthed President Bush and said repeatedly that it was an illegitimate war because they had lied about there being weapons of mass destruction in Iraq to justify attacking them.

I had been at the Pentagon in the CNO's office at the start of the conflict and knew way too much to get involved in a conversation about intelligence with a professor who had no security clearances and was evidently far to the left of my political position. While I worked as CNO N60C in Admiral Tuttle's office, I actually personally did the CNO's evaluation of the command and control systems to support Operation Southern Watch, the no fly zone for Southern Iraq. I didn't discuss specifics with this professor but he knew that I didn't agree with his pronouncements. After a while I got to be known as the "Rush Limbaugh" of the class. At one point this professor presented to me a paper he had downloaded from the internet labeled "Nato Secret" to support his theory that there were no weapons of mass destruction in Iraq at the beginning of the war. I told him he didn't possess that clearance but I did and we don't post those documents on the internet. I knew too much about the intelligence to discuss it with him and let him rant away. He didn't know what he was talking about.

MIT Leading Innovative Organizations Course

I've been able to take advantage of many opportunities that were presented to me in my career. Sometimes it was just because no one else was willing to do them. I spoke at 12 different conferences my last year at SPAWAR. Being heavily involved with the DARPA was a great connection. I was also on the Federal Laboratory Commission and actually sat on the Program Committee for that organization. One of the leading innovation experts ran a course at MIT and I asked to attend. It was a great opportunity and gave me a number of ideas of how we could better transition technologies.

Success as CTO Breeds Hostility

At SPAWAR I had a lot of success. My assistant, Bob Miller, used to laugh that we worked together so closely that we frequently finished the others' sentences in conversations. We did bounce ideas off of each other frequently. My philosophy as Chief Technology Officer (CTO) was that we worked for the guys in the field getting shot at not the bureaucrat leadership of our organization. That didn't win me any friends in that organization. As a result, after 8–9 years of developing technology for the field and selling over $30 million of prototypes to our forces in the field, and paying my own and my staff salaries for the first six years, I was told that I was being demoted to be the deputy and one of my fiercest competitors and critics was to be my boss.. I said "no." They moved me out of my office to a cubical in a classified space and gave me a lower job description.

I appealed the decision to the civilian leader at the command and told him that I thought they could at least let me continue as the leader of the Officer of Research and Technology Applications (ORTA) and he agreed.

My four years at the Naval Academy didn't count toward my military retirement but I found out that they could count toward my Office of Personal Management retirement as a GS-15. I was designated as an ND-5 which was the Science and Technology equivalent of a GS-15 for federal workers. I was eligible to retire with 10 years of Navy civilian service and that bumped it up to 14 years. So in 2011 I retired from SPAWAR.

Moving to Clearview

When you've lived in a home for more than 30 years it kind of grows on you. Elaine was the president of the neighborhood garden club and at one time I was the president of the neighborhood organization. However, there are sometimes some other overriding factors in a decision. Our neighborhood seemed to be somewhat in decline overall. We'd spent a lot remodeling the house and even got one of our friends who did stone work to build a low rock wall out back.

Elaine had worked her magic on the gardens and had 23 varieties of hydrangeas on the lot. I also had six foot blue berry bushes, a peach tree and thornless blackberries. I had even built a greenhouse in the back yard which Hurricane Hugo moved next door. I'd also built a trellis and had muscadines growing up on it. We were settled but the neighbors were not a happy lot. A house was built really close to us on the corner lot next door and they played loud music at night right beneath our bedroom window. It came to a head when the man across the street got mad because my mother-in-law had parked on the street across from the back yard of his house and he got on his riding lawn mower and ran rings around her car throwing dirt, rocks and grass all over it. He later proceeded to stand in the road behind the car when Elaine was trying to back out of our driveway. I had had enough and let my temper get the best of me. We had a discussion in his back yard across the fence and it wasn't pretty. There is probably a good reason for that fence in my mind. He now knows some new terminology to define his canine heritage. He was cutting something with a small paring knife when our discussion started and he immediately dropped it during the initial stages of the conversation.

Elaine's mom had passed away and her father, Dr. Crouse, was over 90. He was in failing health and we were constantly driving to James Island to check on him. We had to get some care givers to stay with him and it was very expensive. At one point we were staying there at night with him most of the time. It's a very sad time in your life when you have to face the fact that you should not be driving anymore and you're now dependent on others to take you where you want to go. We finally faced that issue. Both of Elaine's parents passed away in the home that Dr. Crouse had built and we came to the conclusion that it was better for us to sell our Oglethorpe Drive home and move to his home. We now live in his home on Clearview Drive.

Paul and Andrew Both at Virginia Tech

For eight years we had a boy at Virginia Tech in Blacksburg. Our vehicle had been there so many times that we could hit the road and go to sleep in the back it knew the way. For one of those years we had two sons there at the same time. Both Andrew and Paul got NROTC scholarships and we just had to provide food and other things. No student loans for either of them. Andrew graduated in five years but Paul did it in four. Andrew majored in mechanical engineering. He had been a mechanic since he was a toddler. I still remember him taking his mom's egg timer apart at the age of four and not being able to get it back together again. Andrew really picked out Virginia Tech. We did the "trip from Hell" visiting colleges when he was looking where to go. We were in Iowa when he graduated from High School. We dropped Paul off at Space Camp in

Huntsville, Alabama and went to both the University of Virginia and Virginia Tech. I think we went to UVA first but I'm not sure. We did hear that the VT students had designed the bridge at UVA. When we drove on the campus at VT there was a large common area and Andrew immediately perked up. There were a couple of guys fencing in the common area and he said, "This is where I want to go."

We moved to Charleston, South Carolina while Andrew was at Virginia Tech and Paul had been there a number of times by the time he graduated from High School. They did have a good Computer Science department and at Academic Magnet High School (AMHS) Paul had accumulated 35 college credits before he started college. I don't know if Paul made the choice or we pushed him a little because of Andrew. Paul wanted to go to Carnegie Mellon and we did visit there but he didn't get selected for them. It could not have been due to his academic record, because his high school thesis at AMHS was an 85-page software program in Java that played chess against the computer and he wrote the artificial intelligence algorithms to select the computer's next move. He also did a 75-page paper to go with the program and won the Low Country Intel Science Fair and they paid his way to Albuquerque to compete in the Intel international science fair. His program was called Chess Heuristic Algorithm State Machine (CHASM) for short. He did a great job at Virginia Tech and was asked to be a Training Assistant in Computer science and Math for his last couple of semesters for which he was paid.

Andrew and Melissa got married while he was a junior at Virginia Tech. Melissa was able to get a job at the university book store and they eventually bought some property in West Virginia but after Andrew's Navy duty they moved to Iowa to work for Rockwell Collins. Andrew and Melissa settled in Iowa so we don't get to see them very often. They have three adopted children who are all brothers. Andrew did well in the Navy on the USS *Tennessee* (SSBN–734). He also did a run on USS *Memphis* (SSN–691) to the Persian Gulf to get his submarine dolphins. Paul served on USS *Boise* (SSN–764) for his time in the Navy and he did a tour in Memphis, Tennessee at the recruiting station there before getting out of the Navy. He also made a deterrent patrol on USS *Kentucky* (SSBN–737) as a midshipman.

Paul met his bride, Jessica, at Virginia Tech. They were married after graduation. They now have two beautiful kids our granddaughter and grandson. They also live only 3 miles from us so we see them frequently and enjoy babysitting when they need a day off from parenting.

"Home is the sailor, home from the sea." Robert Louis Stevenson

"Haven from the Sea"

"Have trailer, will travel."

Albuquerque International
Balloon Fiesta

13

ON THE ROAD AGAIN

A silver trailer is not at all confining to someone who has 17 years at sea on submarines.

The Airstream trailer

Elaine got the shingles shot with me at Publix. I guess the shot is not totally effective because she got the shingles anyway. They were severe. They went down the center of her scalp and down her face. She even had a blister on the cornea of her eye. She had to have our ophthalmologist remove that blister and thankfully she didn't lose any vision in her eye. However, the doctor said she needed to destress. That's where the Airstream trailer came into our lives. She came home and said, "We need to get an Airstream so I can destress." So we went to the Airstream dealer and found one. They had new 2013 trailers on the lot but they had one 2012. I told them that they would have to make me a deal that I couldn't refuse. They cut the price significantly and we bought a trailer, a 25-foot Flying Cloud.

We joined an Airstream club with a bunch of other trailer owners and began an adventure. We also joined a number of caravans. That is where a bunch of Airstreams get together with some highly-trained and professional leaders who know the ropes and lead us to adventures we'd never get to by ourselves. They schedule the campgrounds and the events in advance for all the campers. They usually have 20–30 trailers on each caravan. We have now done caravans to the southwest corner states of Colorado, Arizona, Utah and New Mexico, a caravan to the Texas border and Big Bend National Park, to the Blue Ridge Parkway and to Prince Edward Island, Canada north of Newfoundland. Elaine considers the Airstream to be her "happy place".

Selling of the Toccoa Home Place (Reality takes over when you get faced with making hard decisions.)

Because I grew up in Toccoa, Georgia on Ridgemore Drive down on the Tugaloo River, I did not want to sell the rest of the property after Mom passed away at 99 ¾. It really came down to the realization that we didn't have the money to buy the other two thirds of the property from Jack and Jean and we really had no plans to move there from our home in Charleston. Another factor was that Jack was suffering from memory problems and needed the funds from the sale. We priced the property pretty high with water on three sides of the house but the depressed economy in that section of Georgia would not support that price. I still miss the place where I grew up out in the country but refuse to go there since, according to witnesses, they bulldozed the home in which I was raised. Our home had been built in about 1880 but it had been extensively remodeled. It had a hand hewn timber sill in the foundation and hand hewn cross members in the attic. It sat on the last 11 acres of our 255 acre farm on the Tugaloo River on top of a hill. Because the Hartwell Reservoir had been built and covered up all 70 acres of our bottomland, the house now sat on a peninsula with water on three sides of the house.

Clearview Drive, James Island

After Elaine's Dad passed away at 93, we had to do something with his home on James Island. It was a nice ranch three-bedroom home with a fourth bedroom over the garage. There was another issue to also be considered. It was in the middle of two lots. It was not on the water but across the street from the homes with docks behind them on Charleston Harbor. By this time I'd had a number of medical issues with knees and back. I'd had two knee replacements and back issues as well. After we moved I had my third knee replacement. I'd had an initial back surgery in 1996. I blew out lumbar five and had a piece of it sideways pressing on the nerve of my right leg. When it pinched, I couldn't breathe. I had emergency surgery. I'd been on a business trip to South Dakota with Rockwell and had gone to the airport at 5:30 in the morning. When I got to the airport in the rental car, I had a back spasm in the car that straightened me up and I couldn't get out from under the steering wheel. I was screaming in the parking lot. My wife had me scheduled to go to the hospital when my plane arrived in Cedar Rapids, Iowa. I subsequently had two other back surgeries and 13 shots in my lower back. Our home west of the Ashley had four bedrooms but all were on the second floor. That neighborhood also seemed to be in somewhat of a decline. The James Island home neighborhood was on the upswing. After we'd moved the furniture out of the James Island home we came to the conclusion that it would be better to live there and sell our other home instead. So I got to move furniture twice.

Even though a circular drive had been on the plans for the home when Dr. Crouse built it in 1969, he had never installed it. The two-car garage faced the Beauregard Street so our driveway went out that way. There was only a narrow sidewalk of bricks to get to the front door and a dying oak tree in the front yard. I submitted for a permit to install the circular drive on Clearview Drive. The James Island inspector said that Clearview was a state road and I'd have to petition for the permit to Columbia, South Carolina. I submitted the request and was told by the Columbia office that we weren't allowed to have three driveways. I countered that since we were on two lots, I'd put two on one lot and one on the other lot but was rejected again. I went to the James Island Office and got them to write a letter to Columbia saying they didn't have any objections to us having the circular drive. They finally relented and said we had verbal permission and would receive the written permit within a week. Because you had to post the permit at the construction site, I contacted my contractor and had them form up the driveway and get ready to put it in. On Tuesday I called Columbia and asked about the written permit. They said it was coming. I told them that I had arranged to pour concrete on Friday. On Thursday I called again and was told that the lady who had to sign the permit was not in town and couldn't be reached to get the proper signature. I told them that I was pouring concrete on Friday. On Friday, still no permit, so we poured everything except the strip that touched the road for the two entrances. When they finally got us the permit a week late, I got the contractor back out and installed the two culverts and poured the strip connecting it to Clearview Drive.

We put our house in West Ashley up for sale for a relatively high price. We had purchased the home many years ago and had already paid off the mortgage thanks to Dave Ramsey. We'd taken the Financial Peace University course taught by our church and had done the "rice and beans" strategy to get all of our credit cards and other debts paid off. Elaine was a real trooper and we even liquidated the mortgage. Dr. Crouse had built the house on James Island in 1969 and had even cleared the lots himself. There were no loans on that property either. So at age 65 we were debt free. After the sale of the West Ashley property which we had owned for over 30 years, we were able to afford a nice swimming pool and other home upgrades for the James Island home. We made it our "forever" home until we were approached by the undertaker or the Upper Taker, Jesus.

I kid my wife whenever she gets in a bad mood that she has a case of "Aluminumitus." So I stuff her into an aluminum shell and take her for a ride. That's our Airstream Flying Cloud trailer. It works every time. We sometimes sing along with the old song, "On the Road Again". We've taken some really nice trips with other airstream groups. We've been to the four corner states, Arizona, Utah, Colorado and New Mexico. That trip was with about 30 other trailers and was very well planned and executed.

We've been to the Albuquerque, New Mexico hot air balloon airshow with 850 balloons all taking off at the same time with a number of Airstreamers. The last time we were there all of the 150 trailers met at the Camping World in Albuquerque and we had a police escort to the site of the balloon fiesta with blue lights flashing through red lights and all. It was a hoot. The balloons took off less than a 100 feet from where we parked and we were requested to lower our flags to make sure none were obstructing their take offs. There was one enormous balloon that almost didn't make it over the campers. They have what is called the Albuquerque Box there. It's a weather phenomenon that the Sandia Mountains have a cooling effect and the winds go down the mountains. The desert area around where the balloons take off is generally hot and there is an up draft from the heat. When the temperatures are right the balloons can take off from the fiesta go to a higher altitude and the wind currents take them toward the mountains. When they get close to them, they lower their altitude and the wind currents take them back to the launch point. They can go around the box multiple times and land where they took off.

Changes are Hard over 65

We had been at Ashley River Baptist Church for 30 years. I sang tenor in the choir, Elaine worked with the kids in Sunday school. I was the chairman of the deacons for a year. When we got a new pastor, things began to change drastically. The first controversy was when he took the American flag out of the sanctuary. Being a veteran with a congregation full of veterans even back to World War II, that decision didn't sit well with me. I was chastised for an entire deacon's meeting for opposing that decision. I even volunteered to pay for the flag if that was the issue.

He proceeded to come down on other veterans as well. He was upset that one veteran ran an exceptional adult Sunday school class with a very large group. He was also upset with the music director and choir leader. It came to a head when he fired the music director at a personnel committee meeting for "opposing him and encouraging others to do so." The problem with that was that I was in the choir and knew this music minister intimately, and it was totally not true. The other issue was that the pastor had not even talked to the music minister about it. So I sent the statement to the music minister and resigned as a deacon and as the chairman of the personnel committee. I had also operated the electronic sound system for the sanctuary services for a couple of years. This was not the first occurrence of "not the truth" from this pastor. Having handled many nuclear weapons and been in many highly classified arenas, telling the truth is a big factor for me. So we moved from our church of 30 years to another place of worship. We had been attending a C. S. Lewis course at St. Philip's Anglican Church in Charleston for a year but had not attended a single service there. We started going there for worship. I admit initially the liturgical service gave me some issues. However, the pastors were all very good and we started to make some friends there. After we left the previous church the pastor proceeded to fire all eleven people on the staff.

In addition to moving to a new church we also moved from West Ashley and our home of 30 years to James Island to my Father-in-law's home. My wife was no longer in the garden club she had worked with and in which she had many friends. She joined the Camellia Garden Club of Greater Charleston and has found a whole new group of ladies that she has good fellowship with at their meetings. I've been enlisted to make bird houses for them to sell as a fund raiser and at last count I've made 52.

In our new neighborhood on James Island we've gotten to know a number of our neighbors. About twelve years ago we were asked to foster a puppy that had lost the use of his back legs due to an infection in his spine.Our daughter-in-law worked at Pet Helpers. When he came to live with us I knew he was never going home. He was at home. The puppy's name was Claude, but I took one look at him and renamed him Scooter. This was Scooter's first cart.

There are some benefits from living with an engineer. As he grew I had to make new carts for him. In all I've done 9 carts. He loved the beach and we used to go there frequently. He loved to chase crabs, so I installed him a flashlight on his cart so he could find them at night. The kids at the beach loved him and they'd watch him chase the crabs with delight, but had some comments when he ate them alive. He was a great traveler and had been to the Grand Canyon twice with us in the Airstream.

Scooter was my favorite dog of all time. When I sat in my Lazy Boy chair he would come and place his head on my knee. He'd stay there until I petted him. On a caravan trip to the Blue Ridge Parkway I got an intestinal block from scar tissue from previous cancer surgery. I threw up a number of times and had to go into the hospital for four days. Scooter saw me throwing up and leaving. After the second day of my four day hospitalization, Scooter passed away at the age of ten. I still miss him.

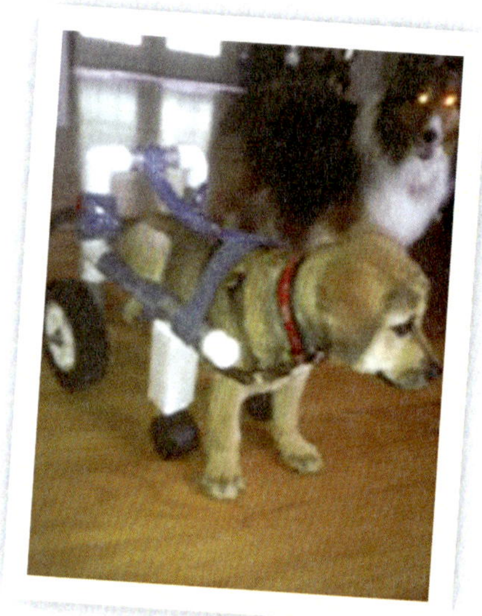

Scooter and his training wheels!

Scooter—all grown up and
ready to roll!

Scooter—The Best Friend Ever

Have wheels, will travel!

Ship's crest, USS *Daniel Boone*
(SSBN–629)

CONCLUSION

What things control your life? When hard times come having a friend like Scooter can help you get through them. When a hurricane hit Charleston, we were travelling and I called my Bible study buddies and they boarded up my home shutters. Who are your reliable friends?

It's easy to start a big project and most of the time it's much harder to finish it. I've done a lot of things in the past 73 years that most people have very little knowledge about. The submarine experience is interesting to a lot of people because, after all, we aren't called the "Silent Service" for nothing. I've not discussed the "classified" things that I've done for good reason. You've probably never talked to anyone who has launched eight Intercontinental ballistic missiles. However, maybe the most important parts of this story are the descriptions of the times I've forced myself to overcome overwhelming odds against success. All of us have challenges.

I've mentioned my faith in God a number of times and have described some of the instances that it was plain to me that without a guiding hand I would not still be here. My life verse is Joshua 1:9:

"Be strong and of good courage; be not afraid, neither be dismayed; for the LORD thy God is with you wherever you go." I encourage you to have a life verse and to believe and live it daily.

I've found that fear or being afraid rarely helps you making good decisions. As we go through a number of challenges we learn more about who we really are inside. Having a strong family is very important to your ability to endure hardship and persevere until the end of a challenge.

Knowing your Savior is always there beside you even in the depths of the sea is even more important.

"I hope you have fair winds and following seas."

Tis The Set Of The Sail – Or – One Ship Sails East
by Ella Wheeler Wilcox

But to every mind there openeth,
A way, and way, and away,
A high soul climbs the highway,
And the low soul gropes the low,
And in between on the misty flats,
The rest drift to and fro.
But to every man there openeth,
A high way and a low,
And every mind decideth,
The way his soul shall go.
One ship sails East,
And another West,
By the self-same winds that blow,
'Tis the set of the sails
And not the gales,
That tells the way we go.
Like the winds of the sea
Are the waves of time,
As we journey along through life,
'Tis the set of the soul,
That determines the goal,
And not the calm or the strife.

My wife did the last two stanzas of this poem in needlepoint many years ago and it hung in my stateroom at sea as Captain of USS *Daniel Boone* (SSBN–629).

EPILOGUE

Reflections and Lessons

- Way out in the country with no neighbors and no plumbing. Was that a bad thing or a good thing?
- It was a big jump from being the valedictorian and star student in high school to being a Plebe at the Naval Academy. I went from being held in high esteem to being treated like dirt in a month.
- Hazing was a common occurrence. Was it really leadership training or just bullying? It taught me a lot about how not to lead other people in the future. It didn't just stop at the Naval Academy, I saw it throughout my career.
- My nuclear power interview with Vice Admiral Rickover, the father of the U.S. nuclear Navy, generated resolve among the strife.
- Make sure the most important things stay a priority in your life.
- Going from being an electrical engineer to being a nuclear engineer taught me that you may never be finished learning new things.
- You train and train but accidents still happen, learn how to deal with them.
- The sea is unforgiving at deep depths. Be prepared to deal with unexpected situations that can change your life.
- Psalm 139 is the Submariner's Psalm. "If I take the wings of the morning, and dwell in the uttermost parts of the sea, even there shall thy hand lead me, and thy right hand shall hold me."

- Train your relief so when you move up you will have consistent knowledgeable support.
- When the going gets really tough, do you cut and run or stand and fight?
- You always need to know where you are going and what the channel looks like to get there.
- You need to pass on what you've learned to the next generation.
- When you are in command or the top level manager, raise each of your team to the next higher level. Their success is your success and legacy.
- Sometimes changes come about for a reason that you don't understand. Go with them and do what the Lord has prepared you to do.
- Mark 13:24–25: "But in those days, after that tribulation, the sun will be darkened, and the moon will not give its light; the stars of heaven will be shaken." When you have launched 8 Intercontinental ballistic missiles with multiple war heads, you must come to terms with the vision of shooting stars reentering the atmosphere and shaking the earth.
- Most people think we are alone but the enemy is never far away.
- Some storms in our lives are bigger than anything we've ever experienced. Prayer and fellowship are what gets us through those hard times.
- Recuperation and strengthening after stressful situations is required.
- Regardless of who you work for, do your job as unto the Lord.
- Never make decisions on major life issues out of an attitude of fear.
- Remember Joshua 1:9.

- We make our plans but the Lord may have other things in mind. I believe sometimes He laughs when he sees what we're planning.
- Use your ideas from your experiences to see innovations in a different light.
- A silver trailer isn't at all confining to someone who has 17 years of sea duty on submarines.
- What things control your life?
- When hard times come having a friend like Scooter can help you through them.

Some sights never get old!

ABOUT THE AUTHOR

Steve was born on April 1st, 1950 in Toccoa Georgia. Our family was originally from England in the 1600s. The Jarrett family was awarded their "Coat of Arms" in 1469 after the War of the Roses. Nine members of the Jarrett family were knighted by the king of England. The Jarrett family motto is "Bravery in Battle." That may explain some of the military background in this book.

Dr. Jarrett resides in Charleston, South Carolina. I wanted some of these stories to be available for my grandkids and the next generation.